TheList Vol. 1

TheList *Vol. 1.*

LANNOO

TheList is your guide
through the overload.

Transforming the mess
into the message.

Carefully selected from the best, sometimes obscure, always smart and beautiful magazines, blogs, Instagrams and online galleries.

01.

What better way to start a book that walks you
through the globe, then with photographer **Sebastian Erras**'
Instagram on Parisian Floors. This is exactly what Marcel Proust had
in mind when he was going on about 'the real voyage of discovery
consists not in seeking new landscapes, but in having new eyes.'
Erras discovered beauty in these colourful mosaic floors
found in in bistros, cafés, hallways and galleries
all over Paris by just looking down. And in taking
some amazing pics while wearing black
Hadstone weave shoes, from Hudson,
of course.

@parisianfloors

Boulevard de SaintGermain.

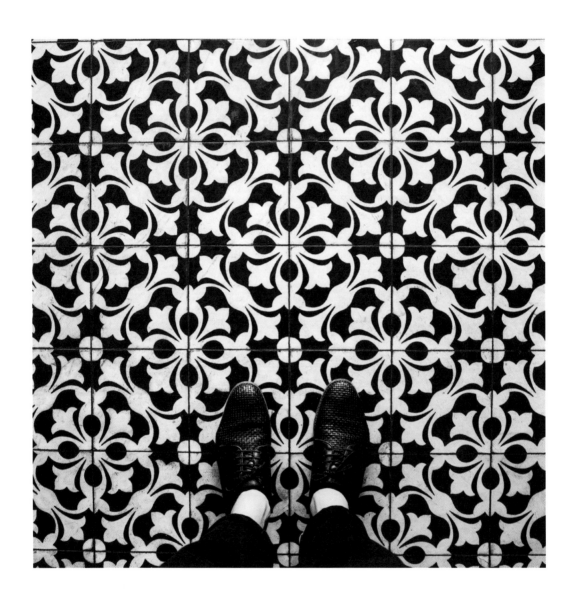

Rue de Bretagne.

Rue Lamarck.

**Genmai Cha Soup with Brown Rice
(serves 2 very generous portions)**

- 1 c brown rice, cooked.
- Your favorite toppings: broccoli,
  edamame, seaweed, roasted tofu
  (below), and whatever you like.
- 2 TB freshly grated ginger (freeze ginger
  for easy grating).
- Tamari (tamari is gluten-free and tastes
  better, use soy sauce if you don't have
  tamari).
- 6 cups of freshly brewed Genmai Cha.
  + Serve soup in large bowls with a
  serving of rice and toppings. Add 1 TB
  of ginger per bowl and pour hot tea over
  everything. Add tamari/soy sauce
  to taste.

Tea Roasted Tofu

- 1/4 c tamari, 1 TB smoky black tea like
  Pu-erh, or Genmai Cha, 3 blocks of
  Tofu, sliced into 6 'steaks' per block.
  + Preheat oven to 220 degrees Celsius.
  Brew tea in tamari by microwaving it
  for 25 seconds (it should be hot and
  bubbly). Allow tea to steep for
  5 minutes. Strain (optional).
  + Coat tofu in tamari and roast for
  15 minutes. Flip tofu and roast for
  another 15 minutes. To reheat,
  pan-sear tofu in sesame oil until crisp
  or golden brown.

princesstofu.com

03.

If you are – like us – fed up with
classic media's craving for breaking news
and the next big headline, you'll be happy
to discover **Narratively.**
Narratively is a platform devoted to
untold human stories, focusing on slow
storytelling, exploring one theme each week
and publishing just one story a day.
From geriatric inmates in the US, resuscitating
a forest in British Colombia, DIY flip books
as an alternative for Youtube, to white
Manhattanites becoming mystical
Muslims and Roy Hayek's
discotheque in Beirut.

narrative.ly

The record baron of Beirut.

By Melissa Tabeek

---

*Through thirty-five years of sectarian strife
and brutal civil war in the Lebanon, a former fighter
and obsessive vinyl collector has provided
a vital soundtrack of distraction.*

Inside a nondescript building with a modest storefront on Beirut's Armenia Street sits a tiny music store, Super Out Discotheque, with a long history. The small space is packed floor to ceiling with outdated but still-functional audio equipment, from a 1970s-era reel-to-reel tape machine and stacks of cassette decks to giant wooden speakers that are more than twenty years old. Thousands of vinyl records, compact discs and cassette tapes are wedged into the shelves, juxtaposed with Christian idols – Virgin Mary statues, photos and several crucifixes – as well as reminders of the Lebanon's 1975-1990 civil war, such as the yellowed photo of Super Out owner Roy Hayek's brother, who died when his vehicle was hit with a rocket-propelled grenade in 1983. Roy Hayek is a garrulous guy with a lit cigarette perpetually either in his mouth or between his

fingers. He is always sharply dressed, thin black hair gelled back, with glasses perched on his nose and a fastidiously groomed matching moustache. On a Wednesday afternoon in May, the fifty-three-year-old music aficionado hums, sings and talks continuously while he burns CDs for his loyal customers. He swings back and forth in his weathered chair, moving from his computer to the wooden counter, the bell above the door ringing every few minutes with new customers coming in from the street. People come here primarily for Hayek's customized mixes and copies of his extensive collection of early- to mid-twentieth century Arabian music. His shop is a neighbourhood fixture now, as it has been since long before he took it over. For thirty-five years the space was his grandfather's pub, until it closed in 1965 after he passed away. Hayek's father wanted to

The Lebanon's brutal war destroyed much of its beautiful capital, leaving more than 200,000 dead and an estimated 17,000 more missing. Despite the fact that the Lebanon continues to be wracked by instability thanks to ISIS encroachment and spillover from the Syrian conflict, there are places such as Super Out that have survived, and even thrived.

continue a business there, so he converted the pub into a store selling Arabian sweets. In 1979, Hayek carried on the third generation of the family business by transforming the bar-turned-sweet shop into the music store it is today.

The Lebanon's brutal war destroyed much of its beautiful capital, leaving more than 200,000 dead and an estimated 17,000 more missing. During those fifteen years, the Green Line – a demarcation of the largely sectarian fighting – divided predominantly Muslim factions in West Beirut from the mainly Christian factions in the East. Once called the Paris of the Middle East for its cosmopolitan culture and world-class architecture, among other things, Beirut itself was severely damaged. Fighting between Israel and the Hezbollah in 1996 again resulted in the destruction of parts of Beirut, as did the devastating thirty-four-day war with Israel in 2006. Despite the fact that the Lebanon continues to be wracked by instability thanks to ISIS encroachment and spillover from the Syrian conflict, there are places such as Super Out that have survived, and even thrived.

This space, which originally dates back to the 1930s, has seen both the country's glory days and the destruction of its wars. Hayek talks fondly of the city's heyday before the civil war but angrily when it comes to politics. Hayek, who started fighting with the Phalange party – a Lebanese right-wing Christian militia – when he was fifteen, lost friends and family during the conflict. Christians are estimated to comprise about forty percent of the Lebanon's population, with Sunni and Shia Muslims and the minority Druze accounting for the rest, and alliances shifted frequently during the long civil war. The start of the conflict is widely considered to be April 13, 1975, when a Beirut bus was ambushed by Phalangist gunmen, killing twenty-seven Palestinian passengers.

Hayek fought for about seven years. When Phalange party leader and president-elect Bachir Gemayel was assassinated in 1982, he put down his gun permanently.

"For us, we lost the cause when [Gemayel] died. Our dream went," Hayek says.

Since then, he has been solely focused on spinning records and selling tapes.

Hayek's prodigious record collection has provided a very good living for him, allowing him to pursue his passion in the neighbourhood where he grew up. Twice married and twice divorced, he enjoys his bachelor life, preferring to fill his days with smoke, conversation and the sound of music. He was just nineteen years old when he opened Super Out – a name he says is inspired by the word "output," referring to music equipment. Back then, he operated the store in between classes at university, where he was studying to be a civil engineer, and before fighting with the Phalange along the front lines of downtown Beirut at night.

"This was where Martyrs' Square was," Hayek says, pointing as he draws the old battle lines on a white square of paper. "We had a bunker in front of St. George's Church. We had another one on the Roxy [a downtown cinema used by snipers]." Downtown, since rebuilt, was then a battlefield. The unofficial front line was a no-man's land known as the Green Line, named for the bushes and other foliage that were left to grow wildly for years while the fighting raged. The heart of the commercial district where the upscale Beirut

Souks shopping center now sits was once the site of fierce battles.

Hayek switches seamlessly from seriousness to laughter as he reminisces about the lighthearted side of being a young man during the civil war. He recalls how he and his friends used to hang out in front of the sandbag-stacked music store in order to monitor who was going in and out, a sack of green fava beans and Heinekens between them. The young fighters used the shop as a place to hang out and rest between battles, listening to music while they talked about girls and drank coffee and whisky. In those days, they listened to classic rock – Eric Clapton, Carlos Santana (one of Hayek's favorites), Genesis and Roy Buchanan.

Super Out Discotheque has survived years of civil war and conflict within Lebanon.

"We used to sit on the wall [across from the store] wearing our uniforms with Heineken doubles in our hands. The Heineken double [an extra-large can] was a trend back then," Hayek says with a smile. After finishing, the men would set up the empty cans and use them for target practice.

The lack of electricity and long power outages

Hayek switches seamlessly from seriousness to laughter as he reminisces about the lighthearted side of being a young man during the civil war. He recalls how he and his friends used to hang out in front of the sandbag-stacked music store in order to monitor who was going in and out, a sack of green fava beans and Heinekens between them.

during the war caused many other shops to close, but Hayek's father worked at Lebanon's state-owned electricity company headquarters, Electricité du Liban, across the street. Through his father's window in the electricity building he got the power he needed to keep Super Out open. Despite the turmoil, business for Hayek was good. He would close up shop at seven p.m. every night, and with all the business, he was able to buy a brand new Nissan off the lot within a couple of years.

Hayek started off with only 100 vinyl records and a couple of pieces of equipment, including the reel-to-reel tape player he bought and the recorder that he still uses today. He was a shrewd entrepreneur when it came to acquiring his collection, driving north to the coastal city of Jounieh, a dangerous trip during the civil war, in order to pick up new records from the port there.

He bought from Beirut's port when shipments came in from Europe, and had a direct connect to Paris through an airplane steward friend who would collect records from Hayek's sister in France and fly back with them in tow. Even today, though he has more records than he could ever

need – about 12,000 – he still has "spies", as he calls them, who are his extra eyes and ears in his eternal search for certain records throughout the Lebanon. Though there are a few other longstanding record stores in the city, Hayek has never considered them competition. His ability to procure difficult-to-find records and provide a consistent source of music to people looking for distraction and fun amidst struggle has always been his strongest selling point.

In an era of online pirating, this self-proclaimed luddite shuns the Internet and still holds on to self-made mixes, though he has evolved from tapes to CDs. Hayek says his refusal to use the Internet mostly stems from the short period of time when he first got online and was constantly barraged by email to send people songs. After a virus wiped out 80,000 songs that he had personally recorded from vinyl records six years ago, he shut down his Internet connection for good. Hayek worships the quality of music above all, dismissing MP3s altogether, believing the only truly clean and real sound comes from a vinyl record. Despite his lack of a presence on the web, his neighbourhood joint is never empty, with cigarette smoke, tunes and discussion perpetually filling the space. The stools on the other side of Hayek's glass counter are nearly always in use. His nearly unmatched collection of vintage Arabian music, copies of which he sells on burned CDs, is still the primary draw. Some cassettes are for sale, but the vinyl records themselves are strictly off the market.

Famous Lebanese musicians such as Wadih el-Safi and Ziad Rahbani have been here over the years, and Hayek has worked with Endemol, the producer of the Arab version of "The Voice." In the past, singers used to come into his shop to make copies of their records – a cheaper option than booking studio recording time – so they could distribute to them to radio stations to be broadcasted.

Hayek is visibly agitated when asked about the recent changes in the area, as his neighbourhood is being quickly transformed, building-by-building, into a fashionable bar and restaurant strip. The neighbourhood, Mar Mikhael, is the new "it" place, and Hayek is incensed with the results. "Everything changed. We used to know every neighbour. Now, everyone is a foreigner. New people come in. A lot of companies have moved

into the residential area...They ruined everything. Everyone is drunk on the streets."

One customer, Marlene Bustros, who lives in the neighbourhood, agrees with Hayek. "Sometimes I can't think of the life we used to have," says Bustros, who has lived in the area for over thirty years. She is a frequent customer who comes in not only for the music, but for the company. She and Hayek joke for hours, with him frequently doing his trademark "moose ears," waving his fingers with his thumbs at his temples while he sticks out his tongue. "I came in for one [CD], now I have nearly eighty," Bustros says.

One thing that has changed for the better, Hayek says, is that while only Christians came here during the civil war, Muslims and others drop in these days.

Even amidst the current instability, it is business as usual at Super Out. As long as Hayek is around, there will always be good company and Arabian coffee on Armenia Street. "There was always coffee on the fire," he says, "Even to this day, it's still on."

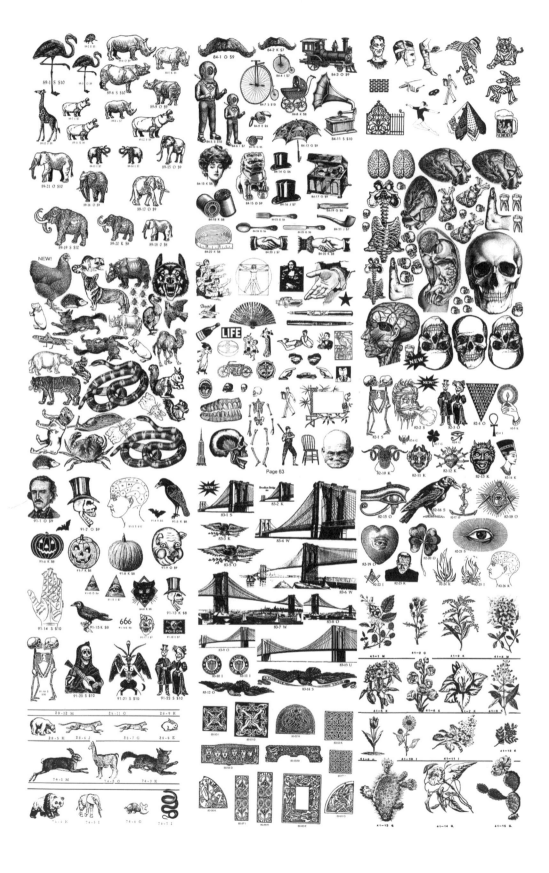

Page 63

04.

You latté-slurping, vinyl-sniffing lot know how to appreciate a broken business model, so a sarcastic Irish guy selling rubber stamps in the East Village should be good news, right?

Even if you're not into rubber or don't particularly need a stamp, be sure to hurry your denim clad ass down to **Casey Rubber Stamps** on your next trip to New York. And don't just Instagram the guy, buy stamps!

322 E 11th St (between 1st and 2nd avenues)

caseyrubberstamps.com

05.

You Can Now Send Your
Enemies a **Jar of Farts**.
The service even allows
you to select the type
of fart (crispy, airy, or juicy),
and write a custom note.

sendajart.com

Will this change the way the West communicates?
We think so. The revenge-by-mail business promises to be bigger
then pickled wieners by this afternoon.

*And then it follows that I travel coming from
the sea between two mirrors.*

*Bent knee of the effective witness diffused
in his streams of paper.*

Irina & Silviu Székely are photographers and
cut&paste collage artists based in Monmouth-
shire, Wales. 'We are enthusiastic sceptics and
disengaged deconstructors,' says Irina when
we ask them about their collaborative collages.
'Cortázar once said: You don't ask a jazz musician,
"But what are you going to play?" He'll laugh at
you. He has a theme, a series of chords he has to
respect, and then he takes up his trumpet or his
saxophone and he begins. It's pretty much the
same with our collage work: there's the silence,
the dim light, the uneasiness of not knowing…
And then we just begin, scissors in hand, those
thoughtless and playful motions of images and
shapes, a micro-symphony of unpredictable
combinations and distortions. An effortless
process that is temporarily disengaging us from
the surrounding reality.' Looking at their work,
their shared passion for Satie seems logical. 'There
is this beautiful tale by Satie from 1917 that we really love: "I had once a marble staircase which was
so beautiful, so beautiful, that I had it stuffed and
used only my window for getting in and out."'

deuxbricoleurs.tumblr.com

irinasilviu.com

The aquadermique horse,
Bataille knows why.

A man of few words, renowned artist Damien Hirst liked
what he saw when visiting Sinke & Van Tongeren's exhibition
in London. So much actually that he bought two entire collections.
The 'La Vie dans l'Eden' Fine Taxidermy collection and
the 'Avis Oxi-Action' photo collection.

Is stuffed the New black?
Probably.

finetaxidermy.com

08.

ASA-NO-HA Floor Lamp by **George Nakashima**

pamono.com

09.

The end of the gallery as we know it.
Pamono is the fastest growing online
marketplace for vintage furniture,
lighting, and interior accessories.
Just a mouse-click away.

Pamono, with over 1 million page views per month since
launching only a year and a half ago, is Europe's fastest growing
online marketplace for vintage furniture, lighting, and interior
accessories. Not only is it an incomparable treasure chest for design
aficionados, it's also the place for smart, original content and engaging
cultural reporting in a visually inspiring format. Entering Pamono gives
you access to a rich catalogue of hard-to-find design pieces – including
hundreds of works by contemporary stars such as Faye Toogood,
Maarten Baas, and Arik Levy and historical masters like
Ettore Sottsass, Hans Wegner, and Charles and Ray Eames, as well as
designs by lesser-known talents – alongside an array of
design-savvy articles.

Ambra Medda's impeccable taste and eye
for bespoke objects of desire makes this
the cream of the curatorial crop.
Check out her interview on the next pages.

pamono.com

10.

Round Bronze Mirror by **Hervé van der Straeten**

pamono.com

11.

The Phytophiler No.2 (Mirrors) by **Dossofiorito**

pamono.com

12. Everyone with a pulse and an accessorised cellphone seems to be a street style photographer these days, so we're always happy to discover those personalties with a real eye for detail and momentum. Wataru – 'Bob' – Shimosato is one those rare talents. 'I'm interested in people that ooze a personal style,' says Bob. 'It should be about more than just clothing.' His **Unknown Quantity** blog is a daily visual treat. Enjoy.

l: Kelly Connor after the Jason Wu show, NY FW15/16.
r: Mikey Kingsland on Mulberry St, NoLita, New York.

13.

'The creative act lasts but a
brief moment, a lightning instant
of give-and-take, just long enough
for you to level the camera and
to trap the fleeting prey in
your little box.'

Henri Cartier-Bresson

Julien Bodet's photography is all about the 'decisive fashion moment'.
"I focus a lot on details, which is very important to me to help me
catch that moment. During fashion weeks, I try to capture the most
interesting outfits/pieces to me, and these moments only last a
fraction of a second, so you have to be fast and efficient if you don't
want to miss them. Just as Henri Cartier-Bresson, the master
of street photography, put it.
Julien's Bleu Mode is a definite must-see for the aesthetically enclined
who are into streetstyle, architecture and backstage snaps.

bleumode.com

Probably not at all what's happening here,
but hey, isn't this the most amazing illustration
of how youngsters feel about print?

bleumode.com

14.

Sara Nicole Rossetto,
Milan, Zona Garibaldi.
Shot by Adam Katz.

le21eme.com

@le21eme

'I think the aim of blogs is to give an honest look at what's happening, however I'm not sure that this is always the end product. There is a lot of product placement and set-up shots done by bloggers, which skews the reality.'

Adam Katz

le21me is on the radar of anyone who's anyone in fashion land. Adam Katz's talent for catching that definite split second that makes a difference makes him one of the big names in blogland. 'Just DON'T call it a street style blog.' With an Instagram that has more views than classic fashion mags around, Adam now travels the world providing the best street style coverage to clients such as *W Magazine, Style. com, Vogue. com, New York Magazine, Who What Wear* and many more. Bookmark already.

le21eme.com

@le21eme

Hanne Gaby Odiele, Milan,
Zona Porta Vittoria.

Anna Dello Russo, Milan, Zona Tortona.

15.

Taking a stroll through the **bamboo grove in Arashiyama** – yes, that's located in the western outskirts of Kyoto – when the sunlight peaks through is better than therapy. It's one of the most popular activities in Kyoto so be prepared for crowds and lots of people snapping photos.

16.

For all you Instagramming, woot-woot-esque, living on the pr-edge bitches out there looking for an Alice-in-Wonderlandian (that is a word) teahouse in the Marais neighborhood in Paris...this is it.

12, rue Dupetit Thouars, 75003 Paris

#lilyofvalley03

17.

'A lot of people don't know this,
but the Empire State Building is
open until 2 a.m. The last elevator
leaves at 1:15. If you go up then,
it's empty, it's beautiful, and the city
sounds like the ocean.'

Zach Woods, actor and comedian

Source?

nymag.com

What do we say?
An insider tip if ever we saw one.
(Re-)discovering a NY landmark by
getting your time right.

18.

A local hipster has been admitted
to hospital with allergic-like symptoms
after eating pork that wasn't artfully
marinated overnight and then pulled by
a middle class cretin.Witnesses claim
that James Harrison, a 28-year-old
web designer and self-described
Snapchat poet from Islington,
ate a burger which he believed to be
sourced from a nearby craft foods fair
only to discover it had been bought
in a branch of Burger King.
"James was fine up until he ate that
non-pulled, mass-produced burger,"
claimed witness and friend,
Tarquin Cockpull, a 25-year-old
entrepreneur who makes hats from
decommissioned tea cosies.

"One second he's enjoying an elderberry craft lemonade he made from his own piss, some moss and Windolene, and the next he's tucking into what looked like a delicious, deconstructed pulled pork and sanguine roasted chutney jus burger."

"It was only as he was biting into the burger and taking that first, pretentious and loudly pleasurable mouthful that I spied the empty Burger King wrapper peeking out of the bin," continued Tarquin, while anxiously twisting the nubs of his elaborate moustache. "I looked back over at Jameso and could see the look of horror in his eyes as he attempted to eat the non-pulled meat."

Tarquin claims that in that moment James began to cough loudly as he attempted to swallow the "regular, chewy meat" but that his throat "literally rejected it" as it hadn't been prepared by an overly earnest artisan burger artist in the back of an old chip van for £9.50 per square inch.

"I should have suspected that the meat wasn't pulled the moment I saw that the burger was being served on a plate instead of a piece of old board," he added. "The chips were just strewn across the plate willy-nilly instead of being kept in a miniature shopping trolley or old coffee tin."

Witnesses claim that as James's face began to turn a bright purple and his lips became swollen, he was rushed to hospital where doctors immediately surmised from his clothing, disdainful friends and ironic t-shirt bearing the slogan "Pull My Pork" that he was suffering from a suspected allergic reaction to the non-pulled, regular burger meat.

"James is just one of the many feckless young fad-eating morons we've treated this year who has, through a sneering disdain for normal food, developed a psychosomatic allergic reaction to any food that the consumption of which doesn't offer a chance to assert a contemptuous superiority over other people," claimed Dr. Allan Marshall, who treated James by administering a drip containing 50cc of Lemon & Ginger infused herbal tea and by reading extracts from this month's issue of *GQ magazine*.

"Usually they're up on their feet after a couple of episodes of Heston Blumenthal and a can of coconut water."

What do we say?
The hipster has – simultaneously with 'the beard' – officially died, and is now the subject of ridicule and irony. Both perfectly executed in this hilarious piece on

wunimdergroundmusic.com.

19.

It's not really about fusion here – it's more about not having to choose, because at Pokito you can have Asian, Mexican and Latin food on your table all at the same time.

Pokito is a place that stops you in your tracks. You'll be walking down the street in Williamsburg with no intention of stopping for a meal, and then suddenly you'll notice something you just can't pass up. The sea foam green doors, that soft sound of The Roots playing, and the charming staff members all beckon you their way. You can't help but enter, and when you do, a whimsical interior and a menu of irresistible little plates will greet you.
The menu itself is also small which is great because it means you can order nearly everything. And you want to, because since one owner is half Dominican, the other is half Japanese, and the chef is Mexican, you can bet the menu is pretty exciting. You'll find yuca fries next to empanadas next to shrimp congee next to ceviche, all of which are excellent and represent their cultures well. It's not really about fusion here – it's more about not having to choose.

pokito.nyc

Found on *meltingbutter.com*

20.

Jenny Nguyen's **Melting Butter** is the online source for curated travel hotspots for the aesthetically inclined. To the point, stylish writing by an international team of correspondents and a great selection of spots. Jenny's hotspot recommendations have also appeared in *The Observer, ForbesLife, Belle Magazine, National Geographic Traveler Magazine* and *Gotham Magazine*.

21.

'A couple of months ago, I spent two days doing some touristy things in Mysore, a city I spent quite a bit of time in as a child. It was nice to discover that even through adult eyes, the Mysore Palace was quite spectacular. On the way from Chamundi hills to the Mysore Palace, we came across a morning market, with tons of fresh produce. A spectacular sight.'

What do we think?
An insider tip if ever we read one. Aysha and her mother founded the Malabar Tea Room, one of India's finest food blogs. 'Our philosophy is simple,' says Aysha. 'Whipping up culinary favourites from around the world in a small-town kitchen, using local ingredients as far as possible.' For recipes and local discovery, hurry to her blog, but we are happy with her report on the morning market near the Mysore palace in India.

malabartearoom.com

22.

Is this the most fun you can have with duct tape, a large cardboard box and a tablet? Undoubtedly.

So what is it?
A cardboard theatre. The perfect set-up to deliver a private,
somewhat immersive movie-watching experience.

How does it work?
Cut a hole in the cardboard box big enough for your
tablet or smartphone. Attach tablet. Lie down,
put box on head, press play and enjoy your private cinema.

Source?
Japanesian Twitter all over the place:

twitter.com/hrhr_mumu/status/416364196389863425/photo/1

twitter.com/exo0814/status/604981487583109120/photo/1

twitter.com/Te2Soccerdamasi/status/604605188532371460/photo/1

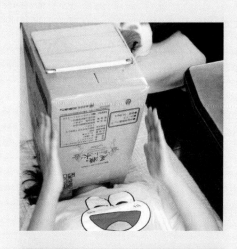

23.

'Women's underarm hair can be adorable,
interesting, humorous, sexy, serious,
connotative and ever-changing.'

26-year-old feminist Xiao Yue in an interview on shangaiist.com

'Believe it or not, but armpit hair is
the latest trend among women on Instagram.
Many have even begun dying their armpit hair,
receiving plenty of praise and criticism
in the process.'

BoredPanda.com

'Armpit Hair Is Trending, and it's a step
forward for women everywhere. If you're a
celebrity, a feminist or just a woman who's
tired of impossible amounts of self-maintenance,
give the razor a break.'

elitedaily.com

Need we say more?
Hairy armpits are right up there with menstrual cups and vagina sunbathing as the
new wave of feminism. China and Miley Cyrus – with a hipster pink version of
the trend – are leading the way, so we're fine.

24.

Ok, so this might be
a little blow (pun intended)
to new feminism.

A Chinese billionaire has locked-in former 22-year old Japanese
Porn Star **Rola Misaki** into an exclusive 15-year, $8 million contract
to be his "personal assistant". While we're sure that one of her duties is
to serve up the booty, the real power move is this guy taking a porn star
away from the public in the prime of her career.

theworldsbestever.com

25.

The real housewives of ancient Egypt had 8-foot-long prenups.

Eight feet long from edge to edge and brushed with beautiful calligraphy, the stretched-out scroll hanging on a wall of the Oriental Institute of the University of Chicago could easily be mistaken for a poem, or an ornate royal decree. It's neither. It's a prenup.

The 2,480-year-old marital document was made to ensure that if the union between the signatories didn't work out, the wife would be adequately provided for. Her compensation would include "1.2 pieces of silver and 36 bags of grain every year for the rest of her life," says Dr. Emily Teeter, an Egyptologist at the Institute.

"Most people have no idea that women in ancient Egypt had the same legal rights as men," says Teeter. Egyptian women, no matter their marital status, could enter into contracts, sue and be sued, and serve on juries and as witnesses. They could acquire and own property (and fairly often, they did: a fragment of papyrus from 1147 B.C, denoting thousands of land holdings names women as the owners of about 10 percent of the listed properties).

Married women could file for divorce, and they were even ensured alimony – provided they had

a document like this one, which they could write up anytime before or during the relationship – at which point it would be more accurately described as a postnup.

Such annuity contracts "were extremely advantageous to the wife," writes professor Janet H. Johnson in an article for the University of Chicago Library. Unlike marriage contracts in contemporary cultures, they were purely economic, promising not eternal faithfulness or mutual responsibility but cold, hard cash. The above contract's annuity ensured the wife could survive with or without her husband (although she had to pay for the privilege, giving him 30 pieces of silver upfront in exchange).

Another, from a compendium of legal documents relating to the northern Egyptian town of Siut, has the husband listing all of the property his wife brought with her into the marriage, and promising, in the case of a formal separation, to repay her for all of it. "One may assume that the woman and her family exerted as much pressure as they could to ensure that the husband made such a contract," Johnson says.

The mechanics of contract-writing in ancient

Egypt were not much different from those in modern-day America. The co-contractors would get together and bring along a scribe and some witnesses. The person proposing the agreement would speak it aloud, and the scribe would write the terms down, translating them into legal language along the way. Then the second person would either accept or refuse. If he or she accepted, the contract was considered binding. If one of the signatories broke the terms, he or she would appear before a court to plead the case. Of course, legal status does not translate directly to life experience. In ancient Egyptian social and political spheres, women were still often dependent on men. As Johnson explains, men fitted into the social hierarchy based on what jobs they held; since many women didn't work, they were instead ranked based on their husbands or fathers. One Egyptian Empire-era text, The Instructions of Any, put it thus: "A woman is asked about her husband, a man is asked about his rank." This might explain why women used their legal power to do some things that seem surprising to us today, such as selling themselves into slavery in exchange for financial security.

Source?

26.

atlasobscura.com is the definitive guide to the world's wondrous and curious places. From miniature cities, bone churches, gigantic flaming holes in the ground to this wondrous piece of ancient Egypt girlpower. Perfect for the mind traveller.

27.

'There is something that happens when you write an emotion down, then leave the words somewhere for someone else to find. It becomes a sort of reverse shoplifting that is both liberating and a little scary.'

Tired of having to be labelled feminist or fashion girl when she actually wanted to be both, the anonymous writer of the **Ambivalently Yours** blog decided to embrace her contradictions by leaving notes anonymously in public places. She is a she, that's all we know. No name, age, eye or hair colour. She can be anyone, and that's the beauty of it. Inspired by the Riot Grrrls and the feminist art of the 70s, AY describes her title as a "refusal to choose between traditional femininity and radical feminism."

What do we think?
Ambivalence being our middle name and with a tendency to enjoy our elegantly combative feminism, we are fans.

ambivalentlyyours.com

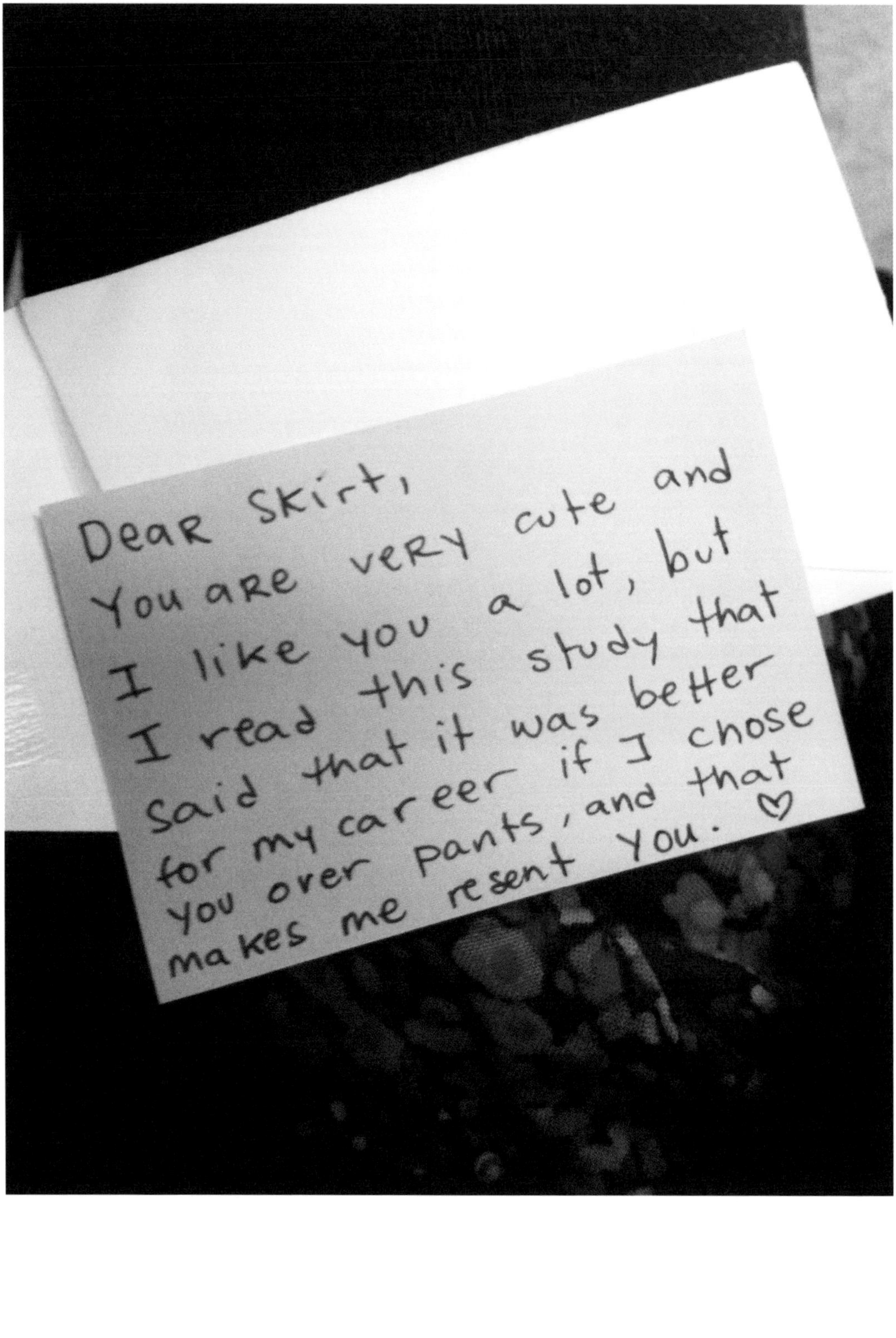
Dear Skirt,
You are very cute and
I like you a lot, but
I read this study that
said that it was better
for my career if I chose
you over pants, and that
makes me resent you. ♡

A note she left in the metro, on the way to work.
'This one was inspired by a study done by the Department of
Psychology at the University of Herfordshire, which determined
that it was better for women to wear skirts rather than pants
when going for a job interview.'

28.

Not only is **Deena Mohamed** Egypt's first female comic artist, she has also created the countries first comic heroine, the hijab-wearing Qahera. The super-heroine fights crime, prejudice, and misogyny. "I made it to let off some steam about a couple of really misogynistic articles I was reading, and it just went from there to address other things that frustrated me," explains Deena in an interview on *Cairo Scene*. What started off as just a fun exercise quickly exploded online, becoming a phenomenon with more than half million visitors to the site, catching the young 19-year-old art student off

guard. What makes this comic successful is the fact that behind all the ass kicking, Qahera's true aim is to highlight the misconceptions of hijabi women both in Egypt and abroad. Clearly a female super-heroine tearing down stereotypes and highlighting the misconceptions of hijabi women is long overdue in Egypt, but we're quite sure that the message is also clear in the West.

29.

Middle of nowhere
officially found.

Deep in the Tasmanian wilderness, in a zone
recognized as a World Heritage site, an old hydro-
electric pumphouse lives a new life as a boutique
retreat. The Pumphouse Point Wilderness Retreat
stands at the end of a long concrete pier in the
middle of Lake St. Clair, a preserved forest in the
heart of the Tasmanian island. It is a one-of-a-
kind escape, surrounded by water on all sides and
located miles from civilization. We'll be there.

pumphousepoint.com.au

30.

These pancake shaped, colourful ceramic plates by **Weiwei Wang** and **Sara Ricciardi** make us smile.

'It's an experiment that celebrates intuition and coincidences,' says Hangzhou born WeiWei. 'Conducted as pure fun, the project was named according to our playful working process – the pancake project. As our experience accumulates, flat, white ceramic pieces grew into colourful plates, each with a unique face. Weiwei, who majored at Pratt University in New York, and graduated at Bauhaus University in Weimar, has been conducting research on traditional Chinese craftsmanship, aiming to find a self-conscious language for the contemporary Chinese design industry.

weiwei-wang.com

31.

Earl Grey waffles, whipped honey cream and poetic manderings.

Local Milk sounds like our kinda food blog.

Local Milk is not a food blog. It's art. Poetic, incredibly honest writing combined with delicious comfort food tastefully photographed by a Southern belle. 'Making the business of everyday living not just beautiful but interesting is my raison d'être', says Elizabeth Evelyn. While some may see a rural landscape showing Beth's recipe for Earl Grey waffles & whipped honey cream, for Beth it is an occasion to wonder about her current love affair with home. 'With home defined as being where the heart is.' But do check the recipe anyway.

localmilkblog.com

32.

'I hate (the word) foodie because
it's cute, like pretty much all diminutives
associated with eating. It distinguishes
the foodie as special because he eats well,
and that's a shitty metric. Rich people
eat better than poor people. People of leisure
eat better than working people.
People with the luxury of choice eat better
than people who subsist. People who
don't have health or ethical concerns
about food can eat better than people
with disease or conscience.
But the cute aspect being tied by
association with that waste and class
makes it particularly repellent.'

Steve Albini

33.

Rose and honey lollipop by Leccare.

@Leccare_Lollipops

34.

Scarred, disfigured, or otherwise odd-shaped fruits and vegetables are the newest status symbols for foodies. Irregular cacti could be the next step.

These pots by ceramicist **Adam Silverman** and cacti by Japanese plant sculptor **Kohei Oda** are the nec plus ultra of potted cacti. Oda's concern is primarily with the personality of plants that he coaxes into unexpected and expressive shapes, typically by grafting two or more succulents into a single, hybrid organism. Many of his specimens are recovered from the waste bins outside large commercial nurseries, which have discarded them as too irregular.

What do we think?

Ugly is the new black. Last year, the French supermarket chain Intermarché launched a campaign to make shoppers see the inner beauty in scarred, disfigured, or otherwise odd-shaped fruits and vegetables. The hype spreads and the ridiculous potato, hideous orange or ugly carrot are new status symbols in foodland. Irregular cacti could be the next step.

adamsilverman.net

Also check *imperfectproduce.com*

35.

If you're wondering what happens when a creative director of big Hollywood movies designs a Mocha, this is it. Swipe the page for the recipe of this Candy Cane Cotton Candy Snow Affogato Mocha.

Los Angeles-based food and lifestyle brand consultant Kristin Guy lets us in on how to create the Candy Cane Cotton Candy Snow Affogato Mocha. 'Dine by Design is my little place on the Internet where I can experiment with flavours, celebrate creative people whom I admire, and inspire new ways to bring a little extra colour and style to your tabletop,' says Kristin. She used to work as a creative director on big Hollywood movies and that shows. The photography and eye for detail have a cinematic drama to them. So here's your insider tip on exploring the cross section of design and food culture AND creating definite conversation starters at your next party.

dinexdesign.com

CANDY CANE COTTON CANDY
SNOW AFFOGATO MOCHA

Ingredients
2 candy canes (or pre-made peppermint cotton candy if you don't have a machine handy), 1-2 shots of espresso, 4-6oz hot chocolate, Vanilla ice cream.

If using a cotton candy maker, follow the specific directions on your machine. Place one scoop of ice cream into a mug and create a cotton candy hood over the top of the mug. Pour hot espresso and hot chocolate over cotton candy, allowing it to melt into sweet peppermint liquid over the ice cream.

DAIRY-FREE BLACK SESAME PUDDING

Ingredients
3 TBS Black Sesame Paste, 5 tsp crushed black sesame seeds, ½ cup granulated sugar, 4 tsp agar agar (or 2 packet of Gelatin), 2 ½ cup Silk Almond-milk, 1 Cup Coconut milk

Bring sugar, sesame paste, seeds and Almond Milk to a boil, stiring until all contents dissolve. Once at a boil, add agar agar mixture and stir until dissolved. Add Coconut milk, stir and remove from heat. Let mixture sit for 10-15 minutes until cool. Pour into mould, (we used spherical ice cube trays) refrigerate overnight. Serve with a dusting of matcha green tea powder.

36.

A Pretty Fucking Good Milkshake
In a blender, mix 1 peeled banana,
1 peeled bourbon vanilla pod,
1 cup vanilla ice cream,
3/4 cup natural yogurt,
1 cup whole milk,
1 tablespoon of honey,
5 ice cubes, and a pinch of salt.
Blend until smooth and frothy.
Pour into 2 glasses and share
with your crush.

Source?

brutalmag.com

37.

Brutal Magazine strives to produce stories that embody
that juxtaposition through stirring visuals,
smart writing, and a sense of humor.

38. *Ceci n'est pas une 911.* You might think you're looking at a mid-70s Porsche 911, but you would be wrong.

Singer Frankestein'd the classic and fused all the best influences from the 60s, 70s and 80s to build this one-off beast. Each feature was crafted individually to suit this one vehicle. Now if somebody would have thought to make this baby electric, we'd be ecstatic. Which almost never happens. The classic body is brand new, with carbon fibre panels and a nickel "targa hoop" above the headrests. The engine is custom built too – a 4.0-liter V6 based on the Porsche 964 from the early 90s.

singervehicledesign.com

39.

'Forget the legends – too many legends – about the fact that you may meet a VIP at Poletti. The only noteworthy things are the exquisite pastries and meringues you will find at breakfast time.'
Rediscovering a classic destination through the eyes of Enrico Grigoletti, founder & editor in chief of **Contemporary Standard.**

Not shy of an old fashioned cliché, we have to acknowledge that there's style and there's Italian style. Enrico Grigoletti's *Contemporary Standard* is the latter. A tailored guide for lovers of art, fashion and contemporary culture with authentic, original content. 'When I launched *Contemporary Standard*, I set myself some goals,' says a smiling Enrico. 'Producing 100% original content was one of these initial objectives.' Be it a story on the timeless classical barber Colla in Milan, Francesca Romana Gaglione proposing the perfect office lunchbox, or Enrico himself guiding us through the streets of Como, it all oozes style. Enrico walks you through the where and who on Lago Maggiore.

contemporarystandard.com

I've never been a big fan of lakes. Deep and cold water, the total absence of sand, and a string of unpleasant memories that involve Germans in socks, Teva in a drunken haze on Garda, and water snakes in Lago Maggiore. Yes, I hate snakes. Then there is Lake Como, a small nugget between Milan and the Swiss border. Actually, it lies beside the road that leads from Milan to Ticino, a road I traversed regularly for work, and so in my mind Como has always represented a passageway rather than a destination.

Therefore, it seemed necessary to settle my debt with the town by providing you all with a series of tips for enjoying a quality day out in Como. You know, just so I could refute my argument and confirm that Como really is a destination worth stopping at, and not just a place to pass by.

By Enrico Grigoletti
Photo by Martina Giammaria

40.

8:30AM
Breakfast at Poletti Cernobbio
Forget the legends – too many legends – about the fact that you may meet a VIP at Poletti. The only noteworthy things are the exquisite pastries and meringues you will find at breakfast time.

41.

9:00AM
From Poletti to Parco di Villa D'Este
Renowned for the Ambrosetti Workshop and annual Concorso D'Elegance that assembles curious folk and lovers of vintage cars, Villa D'Este and its 25 acres of parkland are an attraction on their own. Without listing the celebs that have frequented the place, it's enough to think about Orson Welles, intent on retrieving notebooks from the pool for *The Lady from Shanghai*, to confirm the enchantment of this place.

42.

11:00AM
From Villa D'Este to Villa Balbianello in Tremezzo
Is it enough to tell you that the Villa del Balbianello is one of FAI's (Fondo Ambiente Italiano or the Italian National Trusts) protected sites? No? Fine, here is a brief list of the movies that were filmed inside the villa to convince you. *Star Wars*, *Casino Royale* and *Piccolo Mondo Antico*… just to name a few.

43.

1:00PM
Lunch at La Darsena in Tremezzina
A few minutes far from Villa del Balbianello you can find La Darsena. A peaceful oasis of relax where you can rest and fine dine with an amazing view over the lake.

44.

2:30PM
Visit to Aero Club Como
If you open the website of Aero Club Como the first thing that grabs your attention is this phrase: "The oldest seaplane organisation and water flying school in the world". An accolade approved by the *Guinness Book of World Records*.
I don't know about you guys, but I'm already convinced.

45.

4:00PM
Shopping at A.Gi.Emme and Tessabit
A visit to a city cannot be complete without a serious (even if brief) shopping session. Located on Via Indipendenza, according to *Monocle*, A.Gi.Emme is the zenith of Italian chic. I suggest to only count on Engineered Garments, Nanamica and Salvatore Piccolo among the labels of calibre that are synonymous with excellence.
With about a dozen boutiques dispersed around Como's centre and segmented towards a very specific target market (ready wealthy), Tessabit is able to accommodate a wide range of apparel requests, from well-established fashion brands to more independent labels.

46.

7:00PM
Aperitivo at Pane e Tulipani
Elegant exteriors reflect the essence of this stylish dive, where the atmosphere is pleasurable and the cocktails even more so. For those who do not intend to stay in Como for dinner, Pane e Tulipani is an ideal refreshment stop.

47.

8:30PM
Dinner at Antico Crotto in Porlezza
If you would like to continue your evening, we suggest Antico Crotto in Porlezza where the starred chef Sare Preceruti has re-invented the traditional local cuisine.

48.

Why one of the most legendary celebrity haunts in Paris should be on your to-do list during your next city trip.

The facade of 12, Rue de Richelieu, a nondescript Chinese restaurant ironically called **Davé**, looks like it has seen better days. One could easily mistake it for a questionable massage parlour hiding behind clandestine red velvet curtains; but you would never guess that it's one of the most legendary celebrity haunts in Paris, counting such icons as the late Yves Saint Laurent among its loyal patrons over the years – all thanks to the restaurant's owner and head waiter, whose name is of course, Dave.

Dave Cheung is a legend in his own right (some people call him Dave, others Davé). He's one of those people who has the natural talent of instantly becoming everyone's friend. And when I say everyone, I also mean everyone that's anyone. When celebrated photographer Helmut Newton died, his close friend Davé welcomed a mournful Anna Wintour, Karl Lagerfeld, Jane Birkin, Manolo Blahnik, Tom Ford and 75 other members of the fashion elite into his Chinese restaurant following the memorial service, for some of his homemade comfort food: spring rolls, spare ribs and lemon chicken.

Newton and his wife had spent the previous Christmas with Cheung in his restaurant, just the three of them. Anna Wintour was also loyal customer, having once hosted a party there for 100 people that saw 97 limos parked outside the restaurant for the evening. Johnny Depp and Leonardo DiCaprio took their supermodel girlfriends of the time, Kate Moss and Gisele, on secret dates chez Davé, because they trusted he would never call the paparazzi. It also became known amongst the celebrity elite as a place to come dine, not with their "publicity partners", as Davé would call them, but with their real girlfriends or boyfriends.

The first thing you'll notice when you step behind the red velvet curtain of Davé is how terrifically dark it is for a restaurant that's supposedly open for business. It could double as an opium den for a movie set. The living ghost of Yves Saint Laurent himself could be reading his paper in the corner booth over a plate of dumplings and go unnoticed, hiding behind the protection of Cheung's clandestine set-up.

To enter is to step into another world, another time where you could live out a strange dream you once had in which you dined in candlelight alongside Keith Haring, Woody Allen, Cindy Crawford, Allen Ginsburg and Keanu Reeves – all once counted as loyal customers of Davé when in Paris.

And their pictures are on the wall to prove it. That's the second thing you'll notice upon entering Davé's restaurant; the walls are covered from floor to ceiling with picture frames, squeezed on to every inch of the crimson red velvet wallpaper, holding his precious collection of polaroids that could fill a museum. In most of them, Davé is decades younger, cheek to cheek with the world's most revered fashion, film and music icons.

On my visit, after my eyes have finally adjusted to the darkness, I realise I have not come on a day where I would be rubbing elbows with Leonardo, or Naomi, or Birkin or Bowie and Iman, or any other faces hanging on the walls around me. In fact oddly, I had no trouble at all calling last-minute to reserve a table for two when Cheung personally picked up the phone of this fabled celebrity haunt in Paris – the same restaurant that supposedly hangs a "Complet" (full) sign outside the door even if it's half empty, because Davé doesn't want 'just anybody' coming in. During Fashion Week, Cheung has admitted he pretends to be fully booked for the entire week so he can keep his celebrity sanctuary open solely for his longtime regulars like Grace Coddington, who first led the fashion pack to Davé in the 1980s when the restaurant was located closer to the shows in the Jardins des Tuileries. Then came the rock stars and then Hollywood.

I'm half expecting to meet a rather unfriendly Davé, whose charming reputation for making friends would in fact turn out to extend only to the rich and famous. But to my relief, he's instantly likeable with a kind face and an honest, easy way about him. More of a Dave than a Davé, in fact. Dave moved to Paris with his family as a teenager from Hong Kong and worked as a cook and a waiter for fifteen years until he could finally open his own restaurant in 1982. He's the only one to greet us and the only one to serve us casually throughout the meal. I choose not to say that I'm hoping to write an article on the restaurant and give no indication that I'm anything but your average Joséphine dropping in for some Dim Sum – "Thanks to a friend's recommendation", I respond when he curiously enquires as we sit down, how we had heard of his restaurant.

Again, I found this enquiry a little odd for a restaurant that can name-drop just about any celebrity on the planet as a customer. Surely everyone would know of such a place? But unlike the Hotel Costes or Brasserie Lipp or any other of the Parisian celebrity fly-traps, Cheung has managed to stay off the radar; a true secret celebrity sanctuary, which I can imagine – in an age where a new breed of media-hungry reality stars are out for world domination – is a truly rare commodity. And possibly, no longer needed by the modern-day cult of celebrity.

Which brings me to the realisation as I bite into my pork dumpling, that the reason it feels so

nostalgic here and void of its iconic patronage, might not just be due to the fact that I've come to Dave on a particularly quiet day for business. It seems that Cheung's scruffy greying beard and the empty tables surrounded by distinctly grainy polaroids of celebrities or 90s supermodels in their prime (when Johnny Depp was still dating Kate Moss and before Karl Lagerfeld gave up Chinese food and went on a diet), are all probable signs that an era might have passed at 12, Rue de Richelieu. Perhaps it passed when his old friend Helmut Newton departed in 2004. And perhaps I'm wrong, and when I put it to the test come Fashion Week in September, Dave will laugh when I ask for a table.

Certainly, suggesting the heyday of his pride and joy is somewhat over, wouldn't go down well with the man who gladly gives a tour of his museum of celebrity polaroids to any customer that asks. But I can't help but feel like Davé is just that, a museum of celebrity culture that captures the last generation of true icons, truly being icons – when they weren't so accessible, so overexposed and "victims" of the media. Which is exactly why I think I like Dave or Davé, the way it is now.

Would I really want to eat in the same restaurant as Yves Saint Laurent were he still alive today? It would take away the romance, the mystery, the icon, and he would just be the guy eating stir fried beef at the next table. I prefer simply to know that Yves Saint Laurent might have once sat in my chair, followed by Helmut Newton or Allen Ginsberg.

And who knows? Maybe Grace Coddington or Jane Birkin might slip in for a quiet meal with Dave right after I leave and I'll have missed them by a whisker, which of course would have been Dave's intention anyway.

Yes, I prefer the Dave that just lets me dream amongst his polaroids and imagine which Hollywood legends he's spoken to with the same gentle voice he speaks to me.

Found on *messynesschic.com*
_____

49.

When the **Nakagin Capsule Tower** in Tokyo was completed in 1972, it made a huge splash in the architectural world. It stunned every major architectural journal of the year. The tower is still one of a kind. But today, it's in a state of disrepair, with pretty severe water damage and crumbling concrete. Many residents want to tear the whole thing down and start over. Meanwhile, several owners have put their capsules up on Airbnb, which has given architecture buffs the chance to see inside this fascinating building.

When architect Kisho Kurokawa imagined the city of the future, he saw people ever more on the move, a society changing faster than ever before. Working in Tokyo in the 1960s and 70s, the architect designed an apartment building that would keep up with that future.

Say you wanted to relocate across town. Instead of searching for a new apartment that was right for you, you'd just detach your apartment from its current building, truck it across town, and attach it to a new building. If you got tired of your digs, you could take your apartment down, update it or expand it, and put it back.

Most of the Airbnb listings in Tokyo tend to be either sleek modern apartments, nondescript one-rooms, or traditional old Japanese homes. The Nakagin is something else entirely. "If you are looking for the amenities of a contemporary hotel, this is not a place to stay," cautions one poster. And while some guests complained about the tiny space or lack of amenities, for the most part, it's the peculiar design that is attracting tourists. Architecture enthusiasts and you lot predisposed to quirky digs know where to go.

airbnb.com/rooms/4041371?locale=nl&s=-zKS

50.

This is **Rens Kroes** illustrating
her point that by eating right,
you can get more energy,
look better and feel better.
We're kinda sold.

Many of you will know Doutzen Kroes, the famous model. But did
you know she has an equally successful sister? Rens Kroes special-
izes in healthy eating, rather than modeling, although we think this
Instagram shot won't hurt her book sales. This is Rens illustrating
her point that by eating right, you can get more energy, look better
and feel better. Now where's that cake?!

What do we think?
Genes matter.

@renskroes

hope your performance review went well today!

totally not just saying that because it's my job

"Three years ago, I was some dipshit who owned a used bookstore in Maine. Back then, I was lucky if I sold twenty paperbacks in a day. I was drinking heavily at all hours of the day, and I continue to do so—if anything, my alcoholism has become near-suicidal in its intensity. But these days, I'm drinking out of JOY. That's because I am now an affluent baker of calzones and pizza pies. I wear a big floppy chef's hat and I say 'that's amore!' over a hundred times a day. And I could've never done it without Coke Reynolds' wonderful eBook."

Andrew Jefferts
Deblois, Maine

I'll admit, I was a skeptic. My husband and I are true believers in the printed word—no Kindles in our household! When we were dating, we'd spend whole afternoons lost in the used bookstores around Cambridge. It was a kind of foreplay, really—Harold crouched behind a stack of Latin American history textbooks, watching yours truly seduce some young intellectual for his (i.e., Harold's) erotic amusement. Oh, how we got off. So of course, after opening a bookstore of our own and spending decades as a fixture of our community, I was hesitant to burn all of our books and transition to a quick-'n-greasy sit-down pizzeria. I mean, what did I know about pizzas! But it turns out, there's not a lot to it—some cheese, some sauce, and boom—you've got yourself a pizza. Business is better than it ever was when we sold books, and Harold and I are coming harder than we have in years.

Debbie Gordon
Bardstown, Kentucky

The Hunt for Zuckerberg

The coward Mark Zuckerberg has made fools of us all. To Mark Zuckerberg, our displeasure is exactly like a carafe of tasty wine.

He must be found.

Millions of policemen across the country have abandoned their families to hunt Zuckerberg full-time. But they alone cannot bring Zuckerberg to justice: Your help is required as well. If you see Mark Zuckerberg, befriend him immediately. Then, invite him to your home for snacks and intimacy. Do this over and over again for months. When you are sure Zuckerberg trusts you, call 516–972–3766 and await further instructions.

KNOWN ZUCKERBERG DISGUISES

although lol that said that's actually a crazy-good deal when you think about it

51.

This old school copy-pasted cartoon version of Facebook might just be a social commentary on the evil network's brain-drilling efforts to sell you stuff.

The dystopian Facebook imagines a world where Mark Zuckerberg stole your data and brands talk to you like you're best friends. The Data Drive, the Facebook of a dystopian future, imagines that CEO Mark Zuckerberg has ditched the social networking site and taken all of our data with him. In the wake of Zuck's devious departure, a Texas mattress mogul bought the site's skeleton and is launching a "data drive" to get users to resubmit their personal information. Meanwhile, you'll get repeatedly pinged by Chipotle, as the brand sends you Facebook messages encouraging you to buy a burrito bowl and ask for a raise at your job (because "you totally deserve one").
Dan Kolitz, who created the interactive, alternate reality Facebook had no idea that the social network had actually started allowing brands to message people.

'I'm shocked that that's actually a thing – that's totally crazy to me,' he laughs. 'When I put that together, that did not strike me as a plausible future feature that Facebook would be adding. I guess I was proved wrong, literally immediately.' Any irony using paper and glue sounds good to us.

thedatadrive.com

52.

Social media may be the poster child of
the 21st century, but the ideas behind LinkedIn and
Facebook go back a long, long way.

Alba amicorum were used to establish and solidify personal and
professional relationships of Northern European youngsters of nobility
as early as 1560. They were also used to share favorite songs, reveal crushes,
offer advice, share opinions, and offer comments on other
people's entries – sound familiar?

Found on *messynessychic.com*

Dutch PhD scholar Sophie Reinders is currently exploring how personal books from many centuries ago known as *alba amicorum* – Latin for "friend books" – functioned as a sort of pre-dated version of our modern social media.

In the 16th century, young Dutch, German and French noblemen would go on a foundational version of a Euro-tour in order to educate themselves about the world and visit the times' most influential cities, universities and educators. To record the professional networks, they built during these tours, boys would carry a book with them in which they'd have scholars, philosophers, scientists, artists and fellow students write up a short entry, generally recalling their pleasant meeting and faith in the young men's ventures into the professional world. A full book would underline the boys' social standing and heighten their chances in the professional world – much like a strong LinkedIn network today. Boys' alba amicorum often look very appealing, as famous artists would be requested to paint the men's family arms or lavish pictures symbolizing the well wishes they had for the young men and the adventures they embarked upon. Unfortunately, girls rarely had access to famous artists. But that doesn't mean that their versions of the friendship books were not as – if not even more – interesting.

Girls then didn't have the freedom to travel the world – instead they were sent to convents or courts as a ladies-in-waiting to receive their formative training as young women of high social standing. But that didn't keep them from taking a page from the boys' books (pun intended) and creating their own alba.

According to Sophie, girls' alba amicorum were much more like Facebook than LinkedIn – as they were used to establish and solidify friendships, exchange gossip, and are riddled with inside jokes, personal advice, entry-comments, and illusive hints to secret romances.

So how do these books compare to the modern-day Facebook? Instead of sharing pictures or videos, they would draw them. Instead of sharing an opinion or a newspaper article, they would share a piece of advice or biblical passage, and instead of sharing their favorite song or Spotify playlist, they would write down the lyrics to their favourite song (of course writing a cliché love song in someone's book was the perfect hint that you fancied that person). You could also impress by jotting down some personal poetry, showing off your languages, or getting a little artsy. And relationship updates were done by posting together after marriage.

There were also entries that mirror Facebook "event pages," where guests and friends would write their personal recollections of private parties. The more people wrote in your book, the better you could show the rest of the world that you were a social and popular young lady. And by looking at who wrote what in whose album, Sophie now reconstructs social networks, friendships, acquaintances, and social exchanges from over 400 years ago.

by Inge Oosterhoff

53.

Everyone is interested in what happens
to things when we're not looking at them.
Scientists have carefully studied this problem
and some of them came to a simple
conclusion – they disappear.
Well, not quite like this.
Phenomenalist philosophers believe
that objects only exist as a phenomenon
of consciousness. So, your laptop is only
here while you are aware of, and believe
in its existence, but when you turn away
from it, it ceases to exist until you or
someone else interacts with it.
There is no existence without perception.
This is the root of **phenomenalism**.

Part of a list of mind blowing theories
that will change your perception
of the world on

artthesystem.com.

54.

The **Colombe d'Or** has become a
legendary lunch stop between the border of
the Cote d'Azur and Provence,
serving outstandingly authentic meals
surrounded by the most influential artists
of the 20th century.

Paris has the Café Flore, Venice has Harry's Bar, New York had the Stork Club. There are some places that just had that "je ne sais quoi", a power to lure in the world's most fascinating people where legendary conversations, untold flirtations and scandalous altercations took place at candlelit tables in the corner by the bar.

In the hills above Nice, where the singing cicadas welcome bronzed bodies retreating from the glitz and excess of the Cote d'Azur in need of a sleepy provincial lullaby, one such place awaits in a medieval stone village at the gateway to Provence. The Colombe d'Or has belonged to the same family since it started life in 1920 as "Chez Robinson", a café with an al fresco terrace where locals would drink wine and dance at weekends. Paul Roux, a Provençal farmer, had opened the simple café upon returning from World War I and ran it with his wife "Titti", who convinced him to expand the business into a small hotel as a three-room inn under a new name.

It soon began attracting colourful characters from the nearby region such as the Fitzgeralds, who were summering at their beach villa half an hour south, cavorting with Hemingway and friends in Antibes. Scott and Zelda once had a jealous row over Isadora Duncan at the Colombe d'Or. During World War II, the tiny terracotta hotel became a secluded safe haven for struggling artists such as Braque and Léger, followed by Picasso, Chagall and Renoir who began regularly stopping by for the highly-praised home-cooked lunches. Paul Roux and his wife befriended the artists, and although they had no formal background in art, began developing an eye for it and decided to offer free accommodation in exchange for paintings and sketches. A sign was hung on the door of the Colombe d'Or saying, "Ici on loge à cheval, à pied ou en peinture," – Here we lodge those on foot, on horseback or those with paintings.

And that's how the Colombe d'Or became a legend and ended up with more important art than most museums. The atmosphere of the hotel is thick with nostalgia and the lurking presence of greats such as Picasso, who could be found smoking at the bar, keeping an open tab with the promise of another painting.

His depiction of a flower vase hangs casually next door in the dining room. Paintings by Henri Matisse, another loyal guest, line the walls, a Miró bathes in the poolside warmth, a mural by Legér surveys the terrace and a César Baldaccini's sculpture greets diners at the entrance. Few people actually know the size of the Roux family's collection, nor has it ever been appraised. Certainly at any given time, what is displayed (casually hung above tables and in the hotel's corridors without formal plaques or labels), is but a small glimpse of their secret collection, which rotates like that of a museum. In 1960, a large portion of it was reported stolen and recovered in a storage area of the Marseilles railway station. While the hotel itself has always remained disarmingly simple, the clientele is still anything but. Bohemian, intellectual, artistic knowns and unknowns still head to the sleepy hilltop village of Saint-Paul de Vence for a home away from home. Famed publishing house, Assouline, launched their first book in 1993 on the founder's favourite summer refuge, the Colombe d'Or. The Roux's descendants run the hotel today, still a small-scale operation with under 30 rooms and new works by emerging and struggling artists are always popping up poolside or above a table where Jean Cocteau once worked with Igor Stravinsky on an adaptation of "Oedipus Rex".

The kitchen itself has become a legendary lunch stop between the border of the Cote d'Azur and Provence, serving outstandingly authentic meals surrounded by the most influential artists of the 20th century. A meal on the terrace at the Colombe d'Or may not be the cheapest option in the region, but it's one that will remain in your memory for 20 years to come. Eating fresh fish under a Picasso and a Chagall to the left, you get what you pay for.

Found on *messynessychic.com*

la-colombe-dor.com
06570 Saint-Paul de Vence, France

55.

In Iran women have to cover their
hair in public according to the dress rule
enforced after the Iranian Revolution in 1979.
My Stealthy Freedom is an online social
movement moderated by Iranian journalist
Masih Alinejad where Iranian women
share photos of themselves without
wearing the hijab. A quiet but brave protest
against the Iranian laws that govern
not just their clothing, but the way
they practise their religion.

What's more?
In 2014, approximately 3.6 million women in Iran were warned,
fined, or arrested by the morality police for inappropriate dress, according
to Esmail Ahmadi-Maghaddam, Head of the national
security forces in Iran.

facebook.com/StealthyFreedom

56.

'Do you remember when
MTV played music videos?
Juice VCR is an audio-visual
web station that showcases the
latest music videos and visuals
from DIY + independent artists.
Juice's aim is to help connect
artists directly to new audiences,
celebrate DIY culture and the
hypnotic relationship between
sight and sound.'

Juice founder Jessica Straker

While being fed curated playlists nonstop, it's becoming
harder to experience true discovery. **Juice** works as a continuous,
uninterrupted stream of music videos: there's no search, no choice,
you just hear tracks and get what you're given.
On repeat in The List resort.

juicevcr.com

57.

Japanese women can
now hire good looking men to
wipe away their tears.

If you're a Japanese woman who is having a terrible day at work,
you can place an order for an ikemen to come round. So far, there are six to
choose from, including "bad boy", a dentist and a wise old intellectual.
Together, you watch sad, tearjerking films to get you welling up.
Then, once you're in full flow, the man will place in hand on the wall behind you,
you know like men do in films when they're in the throes of seduction,
he'll touch your cheek and he'll wipe away your tears with a tissue.
The full service will set you back 7,600 yen.

ikemeso-office.com

58.

Red is the new black at Burger King.
After four years of black burgers
popping-up, it's latest bizarre epicurean
creation is an entirely red cheeseburger.
The new red-on-red burger, to be sold in
Japan, is called the **'Aka Burger'**,
which translates to 'red'.
That makes sense.

Is there more?
Burger King Singapore has a black burger and a white burger this year,
while the Malaysian franchise has a black burger called the Ninja.

What do we think?
It's a marketing scam, dear friends. But one with red cheese,
so we're smiling our lips off here.

59.

'I've acquired such a large audience mainly due to patience and shameless self-promotion'

19-year-old **Kate Louise Powell** has shared her Art projects on social media platforms since she was fifteen years old. She currently has over 20,000 fans on Facebook and 40,000 followers on tumblr, with one of her tumblr posts gaining over 112,000 notes. With self-portraits like this going viral the talented teen just scored one extra Like.

katepowellart.tumblr.com

@katelouisepowell

60. **Azuma Makoto** is a Japanese rock musician turned florist-cum-artist. When he's not running his boutique flower shop in Tokyo's Ginza district, he designs botanical installations for the likes of Dries Van Noten or Salvatore Ferragamo, sends a 50-years-old Bonzai tree into space, or constructs a floating, 13-foot-tall bouquet of Heliconia flowers

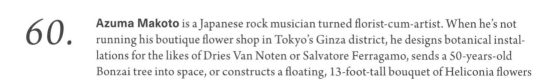

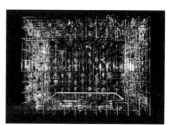

and banana leaves off the coast of Hinoba-an in the Negros
Islands region of the Philippines. Prepare to be dazzled.

azumamakoto.com

61.

'I could eat this **tomato jam** by the jar full. It is that Ah-mazing. Even better it takes a little less than an hour to make and it's so good you could put that s#%&t on everything!'

Adrienne Jopp, founder of sundaypublic.com

---

1 pound tomatoes , chopped,
1/3 cup granulated sugar,
1 teaspoon ground cumin,
2 teaspoons smoked paprika,
pinch of kosher salt,
2 tablespoons lime juice,
1 serrano pepper, minced (or any hot pepper you prefer).

Combine ingredients into a medium, heavy-bottomed sauce pan.
Bring to a boil. Reduce heat to simmer and cook uncovered, stirring frequently.
Cook for roughly 45 minutes, or until the mixture has reached your
desired jam consistency.
Remove from heat, cool, and refrigerate.

sundaypublic.com

62.

'For those that love steampunk products and a cup of java, Gothicism by **Dutch Lab** could be the best thing since sliced bread.'

Jamie Danielle Munto, Trendhunter

Dreamt up by a group of designers who take their coffee very seriously, Dutch Lab's line of remarkably intricate coffee makers is a refreshing departure from the sterile Mr. Coffees and Krups of the world. Their goal? Bringing the focus back to where it should be: the art of brewing.
The metal, glass, and brass hardware-laden pieces come in a slew of styles, with minimalist modern options, steampunk-tinged stuff, and a collection inspired by architectural masterpieces. They each differ slightly from one another, but could all be easily mistaken for something you might come across in a particularly fancy mad scientist's lab.
You don't need to be a career barista to operate one, either. Employing what's most comparable to a slow or cold brewing method, they're each equipped with a water reservoir up top that drips down through a set of meticulously calibrated valves and a series of filters, until eventually reaching your cup at the bottom. It would be hard not to genuinely savor a beverage that's gone on such a journey, just for you.

supercompressor.com

dutch-lab.com

63.

Clara von Wolfchild by **Drew Simpson**
15 x 20 cm
Drew Simpson, a self-taught painter based in Berlin,
produces exceptionally detailed and precise renderings
of a fantastical and irreverent aristocracy.

64.

Sleek-Art is an online art gallery that presents a highly exclusive selection of artworks, chosen by a team of esteemed curators and contributors from around the world. The website is not only an online art sale but invites the viewer into the life of the artists and the history of the pieces, while also providing deeper insights into the contemporary art world. The gallery continues from where *Sleek magazine* leaves off. The quarterly is dedicated to documenting and exploring the contemporary visual, featuring thought leaders and tastemakers from around the world. Just the way we like it. And this is what we bought.

sleek-art.net

65.

L'Amour n'est Pas Libertin by **Edouard Baribeaud**
Tusche on paper, wooden frame with acrylic glass.
41 x 31 cm

66.

Blanco by **Barbara Arcuschin**
Barbara Arcuschin is a Buenos Aires based stylist and photographer.
31.83 x 21.17 cm

67.

Excuse Me by **Berhard Handick**
Bernhard Handick is a photographer who is well-known for his fashion shootings and portraits.
In his collages, which have been published – among other magazines – in *Vogue Italia*,
he creates perfectly conventional fashion photographs and distorts them,
achieving a darker, more underground effect.
50 x 70 cm

68.

'**Other Criteria** makes objects
and books created by artists
to an exceptional standard.
I don't think art has ever been
as popular as it is today and
Other Criteria aims to sell art
to everyone who wants it.'

Damien Hirst

Other Criteria is an arts-based publishing company co-founded
by Damien Hirst. With a gallery on New Bond Street and shops
in Marylebone, Devon and New York, Other Criteria produces books,
prints and editions with a number of established contemporary artists.
Aiming to bring their works to a wider audience of collectors,
Other Criteria places an onus on creating art for all. Not only for
hedge-fund swaggerers with bought taste.

What do we say?
Being one of the most important artists of his generation wasn't enough.
Evolving from artist provocateur to mass-producing art machine,
Damien Hirst has decided he also wants to own the museum store.

There's more?
Hirst doesn't only produce art, he's also a keen buyer.
Swipe the page if you wanna see what he bought recently.

othercriteria.com

69.

Damien Hirst - *Anatomy of an Angel* (white), 2012
Resin, Edition of 50

70.

Polly Morgan - *Sometimes on a Sunday*, 2014
Taxidermy, Green Tree Python, marble, granite
150 x 150 x 195 mm

71.

Damien Hirst - *Glorious Days Glorious Head Golden Magnificent*
Household Gloss on plastic skull
141 x 200 x140 mm

Man Ohne Mund, canvas.

72.

Berlin-based artist **Peter Buechler** likes to
use randomly discovered objects,
particularly banal vintage canvases
and prints sourced from second hand shops,
which he then uses to create new works
by either painting directly on them or
by attaching other materials on to
their surface. His work is found in private
collections across the world.
And he makes us smile.

But why does he call them 'objets trouvés'?
'Cause he makes a direct connection between his own practice
and the tradition of early 20th-century 'assemblages'
of the Surrealists. Duh.

John, 2014. Objets trouvés, diameter 110 cm.

Untitled, 2013. Found objects, randomised spinning tape recorder, 90 x 111 x 25 cm.

73.

'It's the sort of thing you'd
only want to eat if you were
so bladdered you felt the need
to keep clicking your tongue
against the roof of your mouth
to see if your brain could
register the movement.'

The Guardian

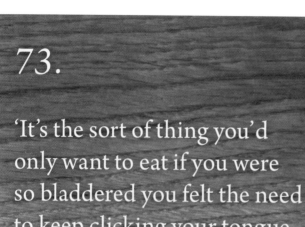

Located on the 40th floor of London's Heron Tower, the **Duck & Waffle** is the highest restaurant in the UK, so if you're up for some superlative views, this is your place. It's open 24/7. Non-stop. Oh, and the title dish is two fluffy waffles with a hunk of crisp-skinned duck confit, a fried duck egg and a pitcher of spiced maple syrup. Not a favourite of the Guardian's critic, but it is an experience we can recommend.

And if you're up for some drinks, check Rich Wood's Instagram. He's the drink guy of Duck and Waffle, and a fierce game changer. @the_cocktailguy

duckandwaffle.com

Heron Tower, 110 Bishopsgate, London EC2

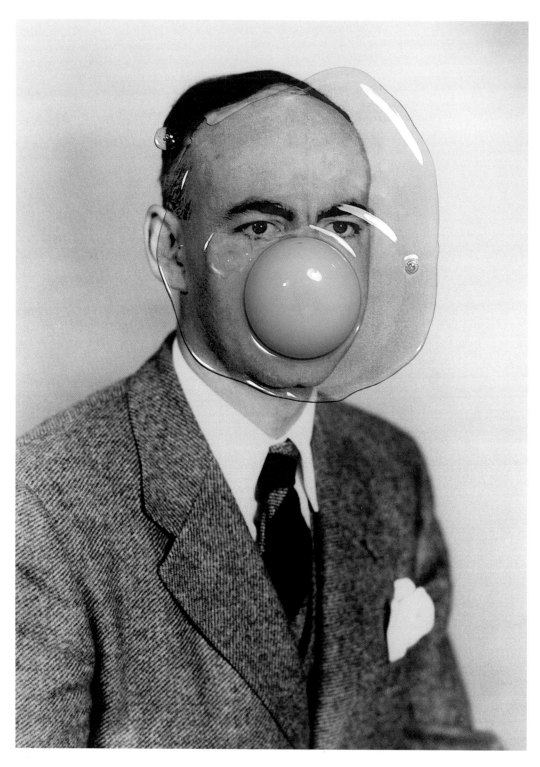

74.   For their playful History and Chips collages, **Rémy Poncet** and **Arnaud Jarsaillon** have
raided the fridge and dressed up classic movie stills and vintage portraits with everything
from smoked salmon and mustard, to ham and pineapple. Anybody up for some egg face?

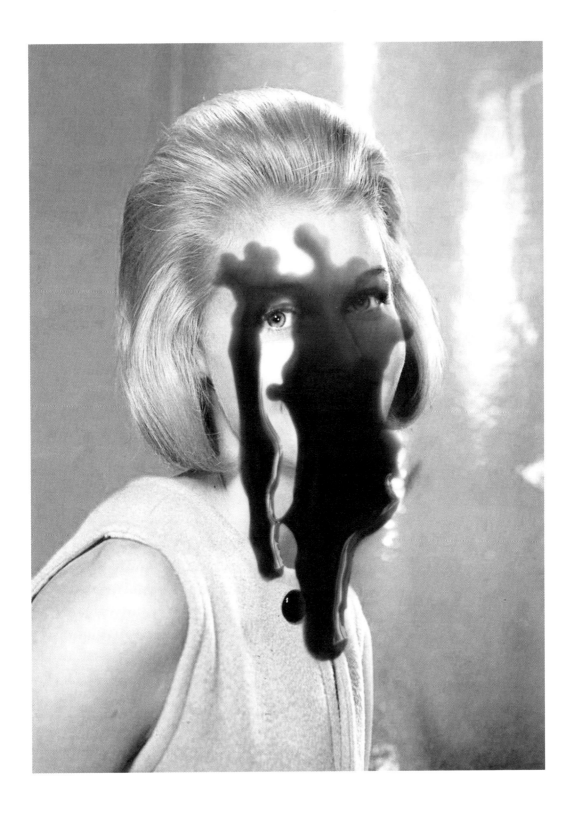

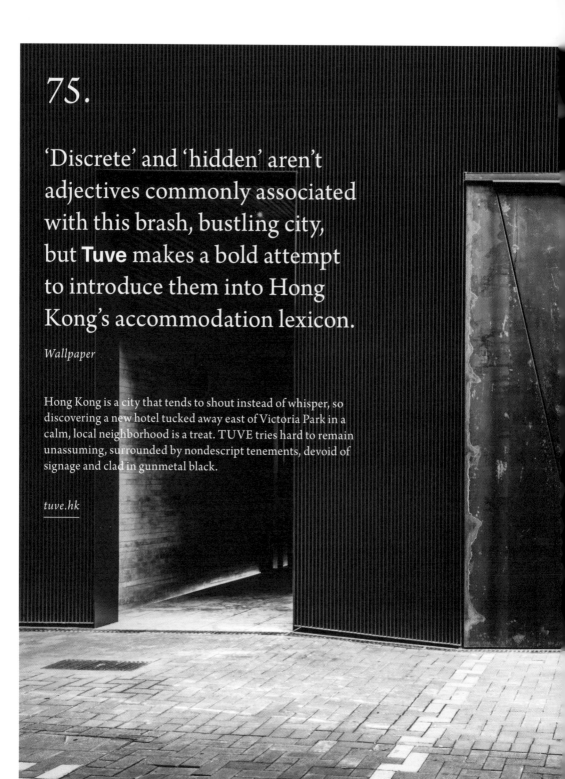

75.

'Discrete' and 'hidden' aren't adjectives commonly associated with this brash, bustling city, but **Tuve** makes a bold attempt to introduce them into Hong Kong's accommodation lexicon.

Wallpaper

Hong Kong is a city that tends to shout instead of whisper, so discovering a new hotel tucked away east of Victoria Park in a calm, local neighborhood is a treat. TUVE tries hard to remain unassuming, surrounded by nondescript tenements, devoid of signage and clad in gunmetal black.

tuve.hk

76.

Huge bookstores chanelling cosmic energy and ancient Buddhist rituals might just be the future of print. The design of the **Fangsuo Book Store** in Chengdu was inspired by Buddhist temples and the scripture libraries that were once housed inside or underneath many of them, and which relate to the Mandarin Chinese concept of stored wisdom.

And slap me silly, call me fruitcake, stored wisdom is what we like most.

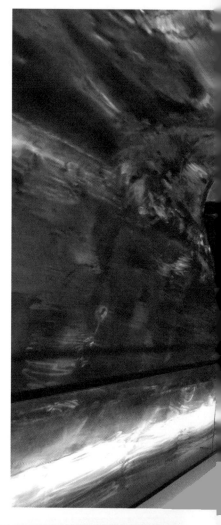

'I wanted to create a modern underground 'Sutra Depository'', says architect Chu Chih-Kang. Sutra depository was a private place for storing all kinds of knowledge, such as books, sutras, and letters in ancient China. A massive, meteor-shaped sculptural entrance opens into a wide, spacious bookstore making the way down already an exciting journey. 'It's a gateway leading to a sacred and unknown world, just like a 'Legend' forever.'

What do we think?
Books, coffee and gateways to discovery sound like the perfect weekend out.

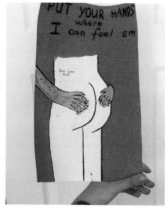
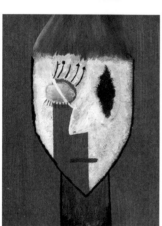

77. New York-based model **Ira Chernova** is more than just a (srsly) ragin' babe; the engineer student-turned-model-turned-artist is a powerhouse of contradictions. When she isn't blowing minds with her dark, spectral photography, she's painting cartoons to remind you how missed your boner is. With over 29.8k followers on Instagram and owner of one of the best t-shirts we've seen in a decade, this is the top model we wanna buy art from.

Sorry, I'm Not Working Right Now

I'D FUCK ME TOO

THINKING OF...

YOUR BONER

indiegogo.com/projects/my-art-for-your-support#/story

chernova.tumblr.com

ira-flow.tumblr.com

78.

Sipping on a traditional cup of tea at the Beijing Tea House overlooking the Forbidden City.

The studio of Japanese architect **Kengo Kuma** has renovated a historical building right in the heart of Beijing, China, using translucent hollow blocks of polyethylene. The new walls allow light to filter gently into the building from all sides. They also rise above the tea house's traditional tiled roof to enclose a terrace overlooking the Forbidden City – Beijing's former imperial palace, and one of the city's biggest tourist attractions. This is where you'll find us after a hard day's night.

79.

'**Wondermark** is created from 19th century woodcuts and engravings, scanned from my personal collection of old books and also from volumes in the Los Angeles Central Library. I'm always interested in acquiring more source material, so if you find a moldy old book in your attic (from 1860-1895), and it's full of old engravings, drop me a line.'

What do we think?

Probably the most fun we ever had with woodcuts. David Malki!
(the exclamation mark denotes excitement!) is an artist, pilot, faux Borat and creator of Wondermark, one of the best comics in the universe.

wondermark.com

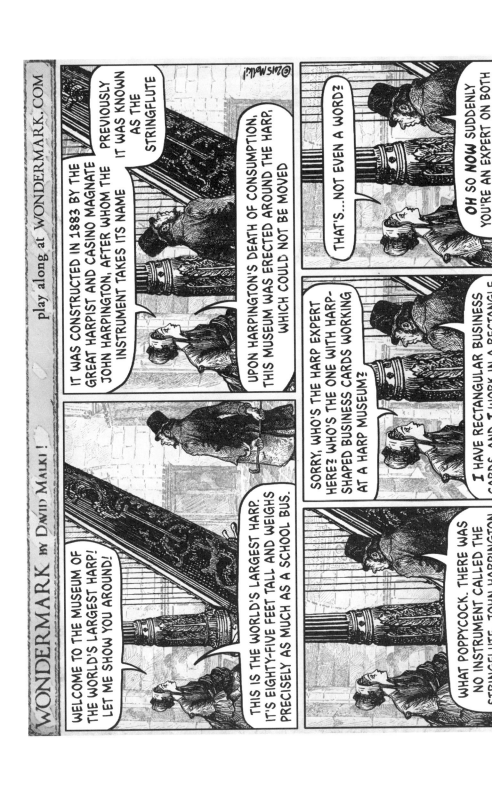

80.

Welcome to the
most inspirational
co-working environment
in the world.

We've never fully embraced the whole co-working thing, but this solar-generated and wind-powered beauty might just help us get on board (right).

Coboat is an 82ft retrofitted sailing catamaran and floating co-working space. Circumnavigating the globe and exploring uncharted waters, It will be home and office for up to 20 digital nomads as they collectively set out on a sea-faring adventure combining life, work and play. It'll be interesting to watch how the whole ocean view, exotic temperatures and natural procrastination thing'll work.

coboat.org

81.

Handmade surfboards drawing inspiration from the Middle Ages? Hell, yeah.

French skateboard specialists **boom-art** have translated
The Garden of Earthly Delights, a triptych by Hieronymus Bosch,
from oil and oak to polyester resin and polyurethane foam.
Perfect for impressing your mildy-pretentious friends.

boom-art.com

82.

The New York-based duo Victoria Rivera and Soren Nielsen are the creators of **Found Fruit**, an ongoing photo series documenting a (literal) cross-section of fruit – the uncommon, the mysterious – from their travels. The images come in pairs, the fruit whole and then halved with precision, and the location discernible in the background. 'As we move from one place to another we make it our mission to seek out local food markets, and pick fruit that is unfamiliar to us. The best part is the first bite,' says Victoria. 'The markets

are always our favourite stop. They're uniquely local, loud and vibrant. You can get a real taste for regional delicacies and everyday life, and getting there always provides an interesting adventure. Quà Gàc was by far our biggest surprise when we sliced it open. It's the red spiky one with the scarlet red pods inside.'

83. In Via Fratta, between the Marche and Emilia Romagna regions of northeastern Italy, there is a small farm surrounded by fruit trees, vegetable gardens and happily pecking hens. Here, graphic designer and passionate farm-to-table food blogger **Valentina Solfrini** focuses on natural cooking. 'A kitchen which pantry is filled with locally sourced, unprocessed ingredients, nutrient rich foods, and a variety of ingredients that can grant

any individual a nutritionally balanced diet as well as the chance to be creative with their meals.'
In *The List*, she serves up her purple Italian Panzanella salad.

hortuscuisine.com

84. Indiana artist **Benje Burdine** turns vintage black & white photographs into scary
haunting scenes. Draw the blinds and turn out the lights; these photos are best
viewed in complete darkness.

85.

The Late Night in Puglia
That Gave Us Martha Stewart's
One-Pan Pasta.

In 2011, Nora Singley – a longtime TV chef, recipe developer, and food stylist for Martha Stewart – was visiting a small former fishing village called Peschici in the north of Puglia, approximately where the spur would be on the boot that is Italy (Zahra Tangorra, the chef-owner of Brucie and a former guest on The Martha Stewart Show, had urged Singley to go there).

One night, Singley and her Martha colleague Sarah Mastracco stumbled into a local restaurant and their waiter Matteo Martella (who was also the chef and owner's son), started telling the two about the speedy way his mom cooked pasta. "I was thinking, 'What do you mean all in one pot?'" Singley told me. "We were aghast. Sarah and I, with all our years of cooking experience – it just completely belied our formal training."

He took them back into the kitchen to prove it, piling everything – tomatoes, onions, dry spaghetti, basil, salt, and a small amount of water – into a very small skillet. About 9 minutes later, they were eating pasta, the unofficial last course of the night. "It was perfect – and perfectly starchy," in the same way that restaurants have a leg up on us with the creaminess and emulsifying power of extra-concentrated, extra-starchy pasta cooking water, Singley told me. "And it was this beautiful moment of learning." Back home in New York, Singley developed the technique into a complete recipe and made it for Martha herself, who was

vetting recipes for her TV show. The recipe didn't make it on to the show at the time, but its next stop was at Living, where Singley offered it up for a developing pasta story. Executive Food Director Lucinda Scala Quinn loved it so much that she turned it into its own feature. The Internet went wild. The rest is history. Bon appetit.

Source?

86.

food52.com sets out to bring cooks together from all over the world in order to exchange recipes and ideas and to support each other in the kitchen. 'We wanted to create a buzzing place for others who do what we do all day long: talk about food, says Executive Editor Kristen Miglore, who wrote the storie on the genius one pan pasta. 'We believe that if you want to eat better, and you want to help change our food system, you need to cook. Maybe not all the time, but some. You don't have to eat local foods every day; you don't have to shop at the farmers market every week. But it's good to try. We're not extremists in a cult of purity, slow-food-ness, or locavorosity. We're realists who believe in applying the best aspects of those food movements to our everyday lives.'

Serves 4

12 ounces linguine
12 ounces cherry or grape tomatoes, halved or quartered if large
1 onion, thinly sliced (about 2 cups)
4 cloves of garlic, thinly sliced
1/2 teaspoon red pepper flakes
2 sprigs basil, plus torn leaves for garnish
2 tablespoons extra-virgin olive oil, plus more for serving
Coarse salt, Freshly ground black pepper
4 1/2 cups water
Freshly grated Parmesan cheese, for serving

- Combine pasta, tomatoes, onion, garlic, red-pepper flakes, basil, oil, 2 teaspoons salt, 1/4 teaspoon pepper, and water in a large straight-sided skillet (the linguine should lay flat).
- Bring to a boil over high heat. Boil mixture, stirring and turning pasta frequently with tongs or a fork, until pasta is al dente and water has nearly evaporated, about 9 minutes.
- Season to taste with salt and pepper, divide among 4 bowls, and garnish with basil. Serve with olive oil and Parmesan.

87.

Move over Kim Kardashian,
Beyond Meat is the most famous
fake chicken in the world, and only
partially due to its list of investors,
which include Biz Stone of Twitter,
Bill Gates, and the Humane
Society. Beyond Meat's products,
which include fake chicken and
fake beef that Twitter co-founder
Biz Stone has described as tasting
"freakishly similar" to real meat,
has about half the fat of the chicken
breast or ground beef it's trying to
replace. And it's cheap compared
to real meat.

'The end of meat as we know it.'
Wired.

'Chicken? Eh sorta. To be honest, I was a little disappointed when it came
to the flavour. The taste isn't waaaaay off base from chicken, but there wasn't
really a whole lot that made me want to keep munching away. Bland? No, not quite.
The flavour is subtle, slightly smoky (I mean really slightly), with just a touch
of earthiness which isn't entirely unappealing.'

vegetarianfoodlab.com

beyondmeat.com

88.

Not new, but – alas – still very much part of Zeitgeist.
This work of Syrian artist **Tammam Azzam** went viral a few years ago.
Azzam made worldwide headlines with this *Freedom Graffiti*.
Enlisting one of the most iconic works of art, Gustav Klimt's *The Kiss*,
to protest the country's suffering, he superimposed a recognisable
image of love over the walls of his war-torn Damascus. Recently,
he has returned to painting with Storeys, a series of monumental works
that communicate the magnitude of the devastation experienced across
his native country through expressionist compositions of destroyed
structures. Exposing the current state of his homeland to the world,
Azzam delves into a therapeutic exercise of
reconstruction, storey by storey.

ayyamgallery.com

@tammamazzam

89.

There's simply no real substitute for
physical presence. We delude ourselves
when we say otherwise, when we invoke and
venerate "quality time", a shopworn phrase
with a debatable promise: that we can plan
instances of extraordinary candour, plot episodes
of exquisite tenderness, engineer intimacy
in an appointed hour. But people tend not
to operate on cue. At least our moods and
emotions don't. We reach out for help at
odd points; we bloom at unpredictable ones.
The surest way to see the brightest colours,
or the darkest ones, is to be watching and
waiting and ready for them.

Frank Bruni wrote a compelling story on
The Myth of Quality Time in *The New York Times*.

What do we think?
Quality time is bullshit. Just be there.

90.

Our feelings – that vast range of fear, joy, grief, sorrow, rage, you name it – are incoherent in the immediacy of the moment. It's only with distance that we are able to turn our powers of observation on ourselves, thus fashioning stories in which we are characters. There's no immediate gratification in this. No great digital crowd is "liking" what we do. We don't experience the Pavlovian, addictive click and response of posting something that momentarily relieves the pressure inside of us, then being showered with emoticons. The gratification we memoirists do experience is infinitely deeper and more bittersweet. It is the complicated, abiding pleasure, to paraphrase Ralph Waldo Emerson, of finding the universal thread that connects us to the rest of humanity, and, by doing so, turns our small, personal sorrows and individual tragedies into art.

A Memoir Is Not a Status Update – beautiful *New Yorker*
essay by novelist and master-memoirist **Dani Shapiro**,
one of the finest writers of our time.

91.

'With digital life, there is the sense
that nothing is ever really lost,
things leave traces and old crimes
deserve to be reconsidered and morally
re-evaluated. It does give a strange
sense that we're hauling our pasts
behind us all the time and asked to be
accountable, not necessarily in a
sensational way, but the way nothing
can be off-the-cuff, there can be no
such thing as misspeaking.
Remember that beautiful time when
you could wake up feeling a bit icky
about what you might've said the
night before at a party, whereas now
everything is on record.'

A quote from Laurence Scott, author of
The Four-Dimensional Human: Ways of living in the digital world
taken from a mighty fine interview on thequietus.com.
The Quietus is a London based online mag on anything from music,
literature, interviews with really smart people, and essays.

92.

Is this second-hand **Hasselblad 500 EL** used on the Apollo 15 mission in 1971 the must-have du jour for photography buffs?

Yes, but Terukazu Fujisawa has beaten you to it.
The WestLicht Photographica Auction in Vienna registered a
hammer price of 550,000 euros for the Hasselblad Electronic
Data Camera sold to the Japanese businessman. Astronaut James Irwin
snapped 299 photos with camera number 1038 while exploring
the moon. Most of the cameras that the Apollo astronauts used
on the lunar surface were left there to reduce the weight of the
moon-rock-laden returning spacecraft. The auction house claims
that this is the only camera who ever made it back to earth,
but some sources claim that maybe four Hasselblad cameras made
the trip back. A perfect mix of controversy, moon nostalgia and
old school tech does make this the perfect gift.

93.

This synthetic perspective view of Pluto
shows what you would see if you were
approximately 1,800 kilometres above Pluto's
equatorial area. Pluto orbits on the fringes of
our solar system, billions of miles away.
Sunlight is much weaker there than it is here
on Earth, yet it isn't completely dark. In fact,
for just a moment near dawn and dusk each day,
the illumination on Earth matches that of
high noon on Pluto. We call this Pluto Time.
If you go outside at this time on a clear day,
the world around you will be as bright as the
brightest part of the day on Pluto.

Check out when your Pluto Time is at
solarsystem.nasa.gov/plutotime/

94.

Aeon publishes some of the most profound and provocative thinking on the web. It asks the big questions and finds the freshest, most original answers, provided by world-leading authorities on science, philosophy and society. Aeon – founded in London by Paul and Brigid Hains – is committed to big ideas, serious enquiry, a humane worldview and good writing. Here's a taster of their thrilling interview with Tesla founder Elon Musk on space travel. Are we living in a petri dish? Bookmark, for God's sake.

'If an advanced civilisation existed at any place in this galaxy, at any point in the past 13.8 billion years, why isn't it everywhere? Even if it moved slowly, it would only need something like .01 per cent of the Universe's lifespan to be everywhere. So why isn't it? The absence of any noticeable life may be an argument in favour of us being in a simulation. If it's not a simulation, then maybe we're in a lab and there's some advanced alien civilisation that's just watching how we develop, out of curiosity, like mould in a petri dish.'

Elon Musk

When I arrived, suddenly, and somewhat theatrically, Musk wheeled around, scooted his chair over, and extended his hand. 'I'm Elon,' he said. It was a nice gesture, but Elon Musk doesn't need much of an introduction. Not since Steve Jobs has an American technologist captured the cultural imagination like Musk. There are tumblrs and subreddits devoted to him. He is the inspiration for Robert Downey Jr's *Iron Man*. His life story has already become a legend. There is the alienated childhood in South Africa, the video game he invented at 12, his migration to the US in the mid-1990s. Then the quick rise, beginning when Musk sold his software company Zip2 for $300 million at the age of 28, and continuing three years later, when he sold PayPal to eBay for $1.5 billion. And finally, the double down, when Musk decided idle hedonism wasn't for him, and instead sank his fortune into a pair of unusually ambitious start-ups. With Tesla, he would replace the world's cars with electric vehicles, and with SpaceX he would colonise Mars. Automobile manufacturing and aerospace are mature industries, dominated by corporate behemoths with plush lobbying budgets and factories in all the right congressional districts. No matter. Musk would transform both, simultaneously, and he would do so within the space of a single generation.

I had come to SpaceX to talk to Musk about his vision for the future of space exploration, and I opened our conversation by asking him an old question: why do we spend so much money in space, when Earth is rife with misery, human and otherwise? It might seem like an unfair question. Musk is a private businessman, not a publicly-funded space agency. But he is also a special case. His biggest customer is NASA and, more importantly, Musk is someone who says he wants to influence the future of humanity. He will tell you so at the slightest prompting, without so much as flinching at the grandiosity of it, or the track record of people who have used this language in the past. Musk enjoys making money, of course, and

he seems to relish the billionaire lifestyle, but he is more than just a capitalist. Whatever else might be said about him, Musk has staked his fortune on businesses that address fundamental human concerns. And so I wondered, why space?

Musk did not give me the usual reasons. He did not claim that we need space to inspire people. He did not sell space as an R & D lab, a font for spin-off technologies like astronaut food and wilderness blankets. He did not say that space is the ultimate testing ground for the human intellect. Instead, he said that going to Mars is as urgent and crucial as lifting billions out of poverty, or eradicating deadly disease.

'I think there is a strong humanitarian argument for making life multi-planetary,' he told me, 'in order to safeguard the existence of humanity in the event that something catastrophic were to happen, in which case being poor or having a disease would be irrelevant, because humanity would be extinct. It would be like, "Good news, the problems of poverty and disease have been solved, but the bad news is there aren't any humans left."'

You can see why NASA has given Musk a shot at human spaceflight. He makes a great rocket but, more than that, he has the old vision in him. He is a revivalist, for those of us who still buy into cosmic manifest destiny. And he can preach. He says we are doomed if we stay here. He says we will suffer fire and brimstone, and even extinction. He says we should go with him, to that darkest and most treacherous of shores. He promises a miracle.

The full article is on AEON.

aeon.co

95.

A shower that feels like you step into a warm cloud AND uses up to 70% less water? Yes, please.

Instead of a stream of water, it produces a fine mist, thanks to the technology that atomizes each water droplet and produces ten times the surface area with a fraction of the volume.

"The last half century of nozzle technology has completely changed what we can do with droplet sizes and distributions," explains co-founder Gabriel Parisi-Amon. "However, this technology has only been applied to very specialised fields such as rocket engines and medical devices. We used these same tools and technology to develop Nebia." After five years in making all this technology has been packaged into a sleek design, that the creators claim can be installed with the ease of changing a lightbulb. Production was funded by a Kickstarter campaign which has raised about $3million of a $100,000 target.

nebia.com

96.

As many as 358 million people in sub-Saharan Africa do not have reliable access to drinking water. Now, researchers have come up with a **book on water safety whose pages can be used to filter water.**
Trials done in 25 contaminated water sites in South Africa, Ghana, Kenya, Haiti, and Bangladesh showed the book, which contains tiny particles of copper and silver, could eliminate over 99% of bacteria, according to results of the project unveiled at the American Chemical Society's national meeting.
Teri Dankovich, from Carnegie Mellon in Pittsburgh, who has been leading the research on what she calls "the drinkable book"

said in one trial, they tested a ditch contaminated with sewage that contained millions of bacteria. "Even with highly contaminated water sources like that one, we can achieve 99.9% purity with our silver-and copper-nanoparticle paper, bringing bacteria levels comparable to those of US drinking water," she said. Each page is embedded with silver and copper nano-particles. The pages contain instructions in English and the local language; water is poured and filtered through the pages themselves. One page can purify up to 100 litres of water and one book can supply one person's drinking water needs for about four years, the researchers said.

97.

Born in France and based in New York, coquettish beauty **Rebecca Dayan** doesn't stay in one place for long. The roving It girl refuses to pick just one city or just one occupation. Since starting out on her own in Paris at the age of 18, Dayan, now 30, has worked as a model, being photographed by the likes of Karl Lagerfeld and Peter Lindbergh; a designer, assisting Gabrielle Greiss at Sonia Rykiel; an actress, most recently starring in the much-acclaimed indie film H_i; and an artist, painting watercolor self portraits. Hot.

rebeccadayan.com

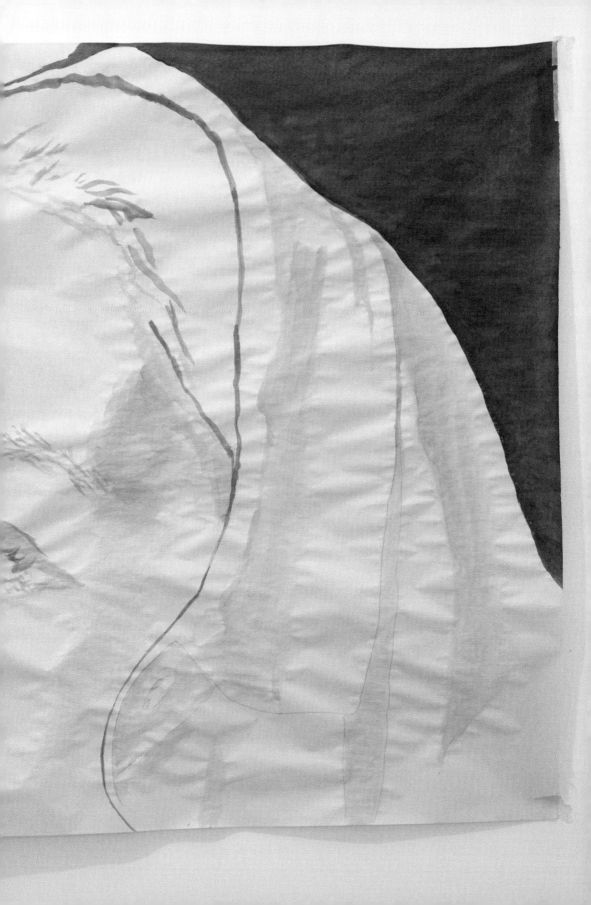

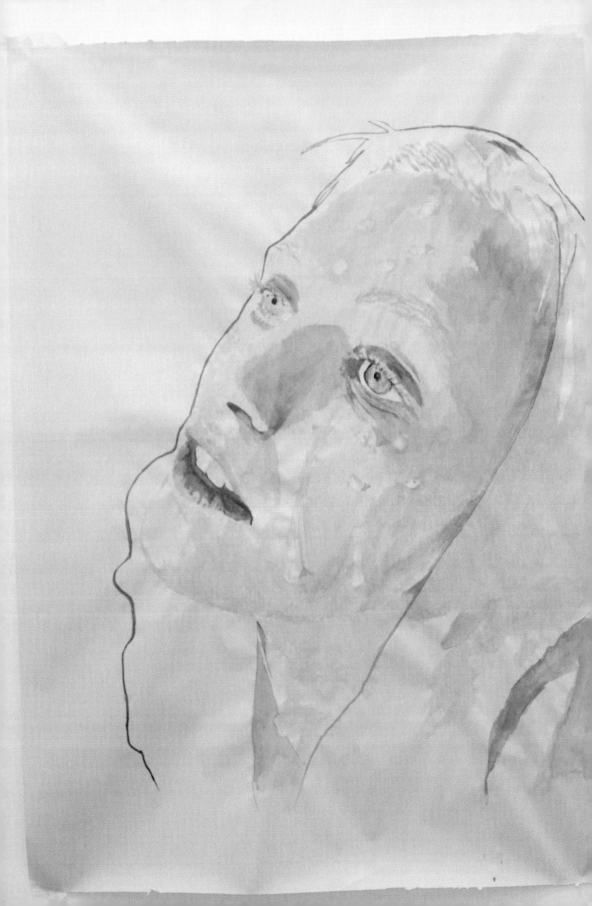

98.

Floter by **Odd Matter** is a container that defies gravity,
bobbing and tumbling as if it is about to fall over every moment.
Using the buoyant nature of cork, these containers are very light
at the top. Keeping them balanced even though it looks like they
shouldn't be. A bit like you, no?

oddmatterstudio.com

NO FACEBOOK
NO TWITTER
NO INSTAGRAM

NO SOCIAL MEDIA
AT ANYTIME

Manish Kapoor s/s 2016.

99.

Online is so last season, darling. A sign backstage at the Alexander Wang show s/s 2016 illustrating fashion's ambiguous relationship with social media. Spotted by our favorite backstage shutterbug Sonny Vandevelde.
Swipe to nr. 100 for more of his work.

Victoria Beckham s/s 2016.

100.

'The show you see on the runway is like a sigh compared to the hurricane that is happening backstage at a fashion show. Models are collapsing from exhaustion, designers are freaking out because the clothes are still being stitched together, and it's way too crowded, but nobody wants to leave.'

Sonny Vandevelde

Sonny Vandevelde's interest in photography started with an old Kodak Box Brownie and his passion evolved into a profession when magazines and ski companies started to take notice of his dynamic action photos of free-style skiers in the Australian alps. Today he covers all major fashion shows around the globe for *Vogue, The New York Times* and infamous Diane Pernet's blog, to name a few. He's renowned for his quirky, stylish, and beautifully shot photography that showcases all the magic and excitement of behind the scenes at an international high calibre fashion parade, offering a unique glimpse into the hidden machinations of the fashion world.

What do we think?
There's lots of backstage shutterbugs, but Vandevelde makes fashion fun. And that shows. Egos are dropped and it's funny faces galore.

sonnyphotos.com

Alexander Wang s/s 2016.

Gucci s/s 2016.

Boss s/s 2016.

Boss s/s 2016.

Schiaperelli Couture s/s 2016.

Rodarte s/s 2016.

101.

Spending summers in sun-drenched Puglia restoring ancient frescoes or sharing daily life with a shepherd is every bit as new renaissance as it sounds.

And that's why we love it. Tonio Creanza organizes art restoration and culinary workshops in wich he shares his passion for the real Puglian culture, history, food and artistic treasures.

Messors founder and director Tonio Creanza has been running fresco and art restoration and volunteer camps for 20 years. Since early childhood, he has harvested the grapes and olives, and planted the Murgian plains with wheat. As a teenager, he explored the underground caves and learned to identify the geographical clues of hidden Hellenic burial sites. His passion for the historically rich region is echoed in the programs approaching them with the enthusiastic concept: 'to do is to learn'– recognizing the importance of process and learning through practice. The sessions provides a practical focus, allowing ample opportunity for participation in restoration technique and creation ex-novo.

Foodies looking to trace the origins, methods and myths of the Mediterranean diet will be happy to learn the social tempo of a weekly structured diet; the pace dictated by yeast rising in bread dough, or the time it takes to make cheese from basic ingredients. "In a fast-paced world supported by grocery stores and an industrial food system, it is easy to feel disconnected from our food. The awareness that comes from participating in this experience is a souvenir that we can all take home to our own kitchens and communities." If you're looking for more than a rustic looking Instagram account insinuating lifestyle, and you really want to get your hands dirty, this is the place.

102.

The Calvert Journal is a guide to the contemporary culture of the new east: the post-Soviet world, the Balkans and the former socialist states of central and eastern Europe.

In a climate where differences are highlighted instead of dialogue and discovery, this is exactly where we wanna be. From art and film to architecture and design, avant-garde culture from these countries has helped shape our view of modern life.

Today, thanks to a rising generation of artistic talent, the new East is in the midst of tremendous change. This is the inspiration for *The Calvert Journal*, which covers the region's culture and creativity through a mix of daily features, news, interviews and photography. Having launched in 2013 with a Russia-only focus, they are increasingly broadening their scope to include other countries, embracing the challenges involved in covering such a large and complex area. Based in London – and with content-sharing partnerships with international titles including *The Guardian, Business Insider, Meduza* and *The Moscow Times* – they tell the story of the new East's contemporary culture via a network of writers and contributors stationed across its many regions and time zones. From the notes of Nelli Fomina, the costume designer on Andrei Tarkovsky's *Solaris*, how the cult of science and space exploration became the unofficial religion of the USSR, how the Soviets stole their best designs from the west, vending machines selling food designed for astronauts at Moscow universities, the new faces of Russian fashion, a photo series on Zarechny, one of the 44 last remaining closed cities left in Russia, a special report on the cuisine of eastern Europe and what it reveals about the region, and an amazing story on what the world's most powerful leaders get to eat when they went for dinner at the Kremlin in the Sixties and Seventies, the zine-cult of Self-publishing, or samizdat, to how a generation of Russian intellectuals became market traders. Time for some brain-travel.

calvertjournal.com

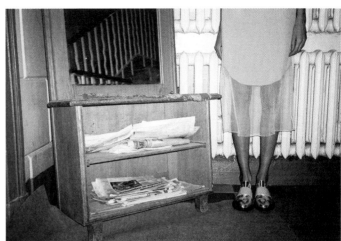

Boris Akimov

is standing
up for real food.

103.

Who?
LavkaLavka co-founder Boris Akimov is on a mission to get Russians back to the land.

104.

What?
LavkaLavka is a Moscow café and a farmers' collective that connects consumers with local producers.

There's a distinct air of egalitarianism about LavkaLavka, a Moscow café and a farmers' collective that connects consumers with local producers. The communal table in the centre of the café is used just as much by employees having their lunch as it is by paying customers. And in the spirit of things, Boris Akimov, co-founder of LavkaLavka, conducts our interview sitting at the table amid the bustle of his fellow workers and diners. In addition to the dishes on the menu, complimentary platters of raw root vegetables, pots of jam, baskets of bread, jugs of cranberry juice, and a large brass samovar of tea are scattered on the table for all to share.

Akimov, 35, a bear-like man with a thick set of whiskers and a mop of curly locks grabs handfuls of the vegetables – carrots, pumpkins, radishes – all seasonal of course, to munch on. "I know where everything you see here comes from and from which farmer," he says, as he begins to point to various foodstuffs. My poached eggs I discover are from farmer Nikolai Aldushin, based near the city of Vladimir, while the side of red caviar is from Murmansk fisherman Anton Iskandyrov. The bread, black from the coal it has been baked with, is from a bakery in Moscow. For those without Akimov by their side, the menu serves as a readily available guide.

The experience recalls an episode of Portlandia, the US television show that satirises hipster

culture, in which a couple ask the waitress question after question about the provenance of the chicken on the menu. They are reassured with a photo of the bird and told it is a "heritage-breed, woodland-raised chicken that's been fed a diet of sheep's milk, soy, and hazelnuts". Yet unlike the US, where consumers' most minuscule of whims are catered to and food choices form a strong part of one's identity, the provision of such granular detail is without parallel in Russia.

Although a far cry from the levels parodied in Portlandia, what the menu at LavkaLavka underscores is a growing interest among Muscovites in the quality and origins of their ingredients. And, it's no exaggeration to say that LavkaLavka has played a significant part in initiating this change. "They have a different mentality," says Akimov of his customers. "Some buy from us because of health reasons, some because they have children, some because they feel a sense of responsibility and some because it's seen as fashionable to eat organic or seasonal food." The company's patrons may be a varied bunch but the price tag attached to its food means they tend to be from the city's wealthier echelons.

LavkaLavka is first a seasonal food distribution service and then a café. It supplies basic provisions such as chickens, eggs, honey and milk from a network of around 50 farmers to a growing number of Muscovites and a handful of restaurants. Ivan Shishkin, co-founder of Delicatessen, a Moscow restaurant that sources up to 30% of its ingredients from LavkaLavka, says he prefers the "honesty and transparency" of the produce. "There's a person behind each product and I'm free to check and see whether it's a product I approve of and want to buy," he says. According to Shishkin, public demand for organic, seasonal food is still limited. "I think it's my role and LavkaLavka's to make more people understand where their food comes from," he says. "Most of my customers don't care but it takes time to change attitudes." For its part, LavkaLavka organises agritours to member farms as well as other food-related events, such as a monthly farmers' show-and-tell for children and regular lectures by the famous Russian food writer Maksim Syrnikov; all are designed to encourage consumers to think about the food they eat and where it comes from.

LavkaLavka takes an equally conscientious approach when selecting its farmers, admitting only those who meet its strict criteria into its circle. Farmers must, for instance, observe good animal welfare practices and broadly speaking, be "organic" (Russia does not yet have a certified labelling scheme for food produced organically, giving rise to fast and loose definitions). "They have opened a market for us that did not exist before," says John Kopiski, a dairy and beef farmer who is in the process of joining the LavkaLavka family

Akimov, 35, a bear-like man with a thick set of whiskers and a mop of curly locks grabs handfuls of the vegetables – carrots, pumpkins, radishes – all seasonal of course, to munch on. "I know where everything you see here comes from and from which farmer," he says, as he begins to point to various foodstuffs. My poached eggs I discover are from farmer Nikolai Aldushin, based near the city of Vladimir, while the side of red caviar is from Murmansk fisherman Anton Iskandyrov. The bread, black from the coal it has been baked with, is from a bakery in Moscow. For those without Akimov by their side, the menu serves as readily available guide.

The experience recalls an episode of Portlandia, the US television show that satirises hipster culture, in which a couple ask the waitress question after question about the provenance of the chicken on the menu. They are reassured with a photo of the bird and told it is a "heritage-breed, woodland-raised chicken that's been fed a diet of sheep's milk, soy, and hazelnuts". Yet unlike the US, where consumers' most minuscule of whims are catered to and food choices form a strong part of one's identity, the provision of such granular detail is without parallel in Russia.

'In Russia, they're considered to be peasants who are trying to move to Moscow but can't. We want to change that thinking and make farming a respected profession.'

as a supplier of bottled milk, yoghurt and cheese. "To develop an image and product in any market takes time and resources and LavkaLavka have invested in this part of the market. A farmer that has a partner that provides market knowledge can help the farmer develop."

Akimov did not originally set out to help small- to medium-sized farmers establish themselves or to introduce the concept of virtuous food to Muscovites. When he launched LavkaLavka (lavka means shop in Russian) with his business partner Alexander Mikhail, 37, in 2009, the two cooking enthusiasts (and former members of industrial avant-garde band Inquisitorum) were simply after high-quality ingredients. The company's first incarnation was a no-frills page on *LiveJournal*, a popular blogging platform in Russia. The message on the page was simple: "We're buying geese and butter from these farmers. Do you want some?" "The idea was really just to feed ourselves," says Akimov, who was working as a journalist at the time, a career he embarked on at the age of 19.

As LavkaLavka's reputation grew, so did its customer base and in 2010, it moved to its current spot in the Arma factory complex, an old gasworks behind Kursky station. Along the way, its purpose has gradually evolved into something loftier. The assistance that it now provides to farmers is part of a wider agenda to change prevailing attitudes towards farming. "It's not like in Europe or in the US where farmers are respected," he says. "In Russia, they're considered to be peasants who are trying to move to Moscow but can't. We want to change that thinking and make farming a respected profession."

This kind of thinking can be traced back to the agricultural policy of the early Soviet era when peasants were bundled into collective farms in an attempt to boost efficiency. The result was enmity towards the state among farmers, whose movements were severely restricted, and a succession of famines. It wasn't until the collapse of the Soviet Union in 1991 that forced collectivisation ended, bringing with it rural flight and years of agricultural decline. The industry has since picked up, but undoing years of Soviet mismanagement has been a painfully slow process. According to the World Food Programme, Russia has more fertile yet fallow land than anywhere else in the world. The upshot is that Russia is a net importer of food, including beef, pork, chicken and cheese. "In terms of farming, around 70% to 80% of all our vegetables come from other countries," says Akimov. "There's lots of land. We have this huge territory but we don't use it."

For Akimov, reversing the migratory trends of the past two decades by inspiring a generation of urbanites to give up their turbocharged lifestyles and move back to the land is one solution. Among LavkaLavka's farmers, he says, are a number of former city professionals including a journalist, an art dealer and a ballet director. "The main problem is that you don't see people in the middle of Russia," he says. "Our idea is that people from the cities should move back."

Akimov's cri de coeur is not just practical: the past few years have kindled a profound and personal appreciation of the Russian country-side within him. Although he has a busy few years ahead of him with plans to open up more branches of LavkaLavka, a farmer's market and a restaurant, he dreams of heading to Karelia, a region in northern Russian that runs along the Finnish border, where he has a house on an island with a big lake. Until then, he'll make do with spending as much time in Russia's great outdoors. "I have five homes all over the country," he says. "Old traditional houses in beautiful surroundings in villages with totally different lifestyles. I think if I buy a house and spend even just several days a year there then I'll be touching another reality and that excites me."

105.

'The fundamental nature of news journalism
has changed for the worst in the last
twenty years. Almost without anybody
noticing. Many of the things we looked
at journalists to provide us with – accuracy,
impartiality, context, depth – are all under
threat. The antidote comes in the form of a
new slow journalism revolution.'

Delayed Gratification founder, Rob Orchard

Delayed Gratification is a quarterly publication which revisits the events of the previous three months to see what has happened after the dust has settled and the news agenda has moved on. They report on the events that mattered through glorious infographics, extraordinary photo features and long-form journalism. Did you hear the one about the Welsh terrorist who tried to blow up the Prince of Wales's investiture? Or Saddam Hussein's epic propaganda movie featuring Oliver Reed? Perhaps you'd be interested in a behind-the-scenes view of the English Defence League? Or the story of the electrical engineer from Derby who became a king in Nigeria? Time for a chat.

Does slow journalism stand a chance against our addiction to the instant gratification of newsporn?

'We've always maintained that Slow Journalism isn't an alternative to fast media, but an important supplement. With *Delayed Gratification*, we hope to give people who devour news on a daily basis a three-monthly opportunity to zoom out and look back on the headlines that have dominated the news: Which events actually mattered? Which ones were synthetic and PR-driven? Ultimately, we do think this type of reflection is important in building media literacy, and getting better at assessing when instant news reports and social media wildfires should be taken with a grain of salt. Now more than ever, it's important that people recognise what's good reporting and what's fluff, or flat-out inaccuracy. By seeing the discrepancies between immediate news reports and slower coverage, it becomes easier to read between the lines of fast news.

Where did newspapers go wrong?

'Newspapers have worked very hard to cope with the technological advances that pretty much destroyed their business model, so it's not really fair to say they went down a wrong path. We're still in a transitional phase where the news media are learning how to operate in a time when mass communication is instant. This imperative to beat every single person on the Internet to the chase and be first to break a story is a bad idea though – it's just so conducive to inaccuracies, as well as being extremely difficult. When Amy Winehouse died, for example, the news broke on Twitter 20 minutes after the police were called. By the time mainstream media confirmed the story, 40 minutes had passed and 20 million people had already tweeted about it. Some news media are going in the opposite direction though, focusing more on interpreting and explaining news events. That's very encouraging.'

How important are the infographics?

They are very important to us. Data visualisation allows us to capture very complex stories within a double-page spread. What's interesting about infographics versus words is that you can be comprehensive as well as pointing out the interesting outliers. In written journalism, the outliers get most of the attention because what's news is often what's unusual. In our infographics, we try to convey the most surprising facts about the data sets we use, while at the same time showing how these fit into the bigger picture.

The infographic on *Vogue* is an eye-opener. Is that illustration of an alienation part of the end of print?

'We are sometimes a bit weary of magazines which aim to be 'aspirational'. To us non-A-listers, 'aspirational' usually just means 'unattainable', and immersing yourself in pictures of stuff you'll never own, or places you'll never go to, can induce quite a bit of anxiety. With the *Vogue* infographic, we wanted to show just how unrealistically expensive some of the fashion promoted in high-end magazines is. One of our favourite things in the infographic is the single poncho which goes for £3,654. You could almost get a Master's degree for that money. Or you could spend it on a poncho.'

Check out the next pages for some amazing examples of the *Delayed Gratification* infographics. And get yourself a subscription. Fast.

slow-journalism.com

VOGUE

Dresses and skirts
£213,560

Dresses £186,342
Skirts £27,218

Embroidered silk maxi dress, Dior £26,000 p393

Coats and jackets
£120,855

Coats £71,526
Jackets/blazers £41,075
Ponchos £3,654 | Capes £3,545
Gilets/vests £1,055

Tops £38,927

Bustiers £32,385 | Shirts £3,529
Blouses £1,979
T-shirts £1,035

Jewellery and watches
£141,613

Rings £37,535

Bracelets £30,430

Stephen Webster citrine, amethyst, garnet, topaz, peridot and diamond necklace £70,000 p288

Earrings £1,824

Other necklaces/pendants £1,239

Watches £585

Footwear
£44,841

Boots £30,345
Shoes £14,496

Jumpers £28,083

Sweaters £14,268

Polo/Turtle necks £8,428

Cardigans/track tops £5,387

Accessories
£35,290

Bags £22,327 | Belts £3,839

Scarfs £3,551

Clutches £2,694

Sunglasses £2,096

Miscellaneous £783

Trousers
£12,824

Smart £8,140

Jeans/leggings/shorts/jumpsuits £4,684

Cosmetics £2,720

Total value of products featured £638,713

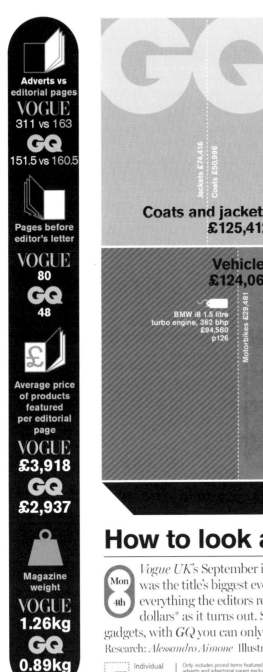

Adverts vs editorial pages

VOGUE
311 vs 163

GQ
151.5 vs 160.5

Pages before editor's letter

VOGUE
80

GQ
48

Average price of products featured per editorial page

VOGUE
£3,918

GQ
£2,937

Magazine weight

VOGUE
1.26kg

GQ
0.89kg

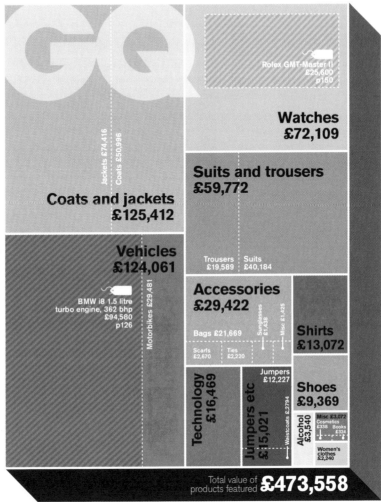

Rolex GMT-Master II
£25,600
p150

Watches £72,109

Suits and trousers £59,772

Jackets £74,416 — Coats £50,996

Coats and jackets £125,412

Vehicles £124,061

Trousers £19,589 | Suits £40,184

BMW i8 1.5 litre turbo engine, 362 bhp £94,580 p126

Motorbikes £29,481

Accessories £29,422

Sunglasses £1,438 | Misc £1,425

Bags £21,669

Shirts £13,072

Scarfs £2,670 | Ties £2,220

Jumpers £12,227

Technology £16,469

Jumpers etc £15,021

Waistcoats £2,794

Shoes £9,369

Alcohol £3,540

Misc £3,072
Cosmetics £338 | Books £324

Women's clothes £2,240

Total value of products featured **£473,558**

How to look a million dollars

Mon 8 4th

Vogue UK's September issue, which came out on 4th August, was the title's biggest ever. But how much would it cost to buy everything the editors recommended? Almost exactly a million dollars* as it turns out. Sorry gents: even throwing in its cars and gadgets, with *GQ* you can only look $741,219. Here's how it breaks down

Research: *Alessandro Aimone* Illustration: *Christian Tate*

Individual high ticket items

Only includes priced items featured in editorial pages; adverts and advertorial pages excluded.

* The exact total in dollars is $999,722, based on a representative September 2014 exchange rate

Jan

Russia passes new regulations which see transsexuals and transvestites banned from driving. The new laws also include exhibitionism and voyeurism as "mental disorders" which lead to unsafe driving.

Thu 8th

Officials in northern Nigeria report thousands of people missing after **Islamist group Boko Haram raids several towns and villages.** Up to 2,000 people are feared dead.

"Here comes Willie... he has no pants"

A song in a cartoon on a Swedish kids' TV programme is heavily criticised for featuring dancing genitals. *Bacillakuten*, a show on children's TV channel Barnkanalen, says its aim is to educate children about the human body.

Saudi blogger Raif Badawi receives his first public flogging in Jeddah having been convicted of insulting Islam. He was sentenced in May 2014 to ten years in prison and 1,000 lashes. Authorities plan to administer the lashes in sets of 50 over a course of 20 weeks.

Fri 9th

Fri 23rd

Judge J Paul Oetken of the US district court in Manhattan rules that Haitians are not able to sue the UN for a cholera epidemic in their country.

Sri Lanka's new president pledges to end authoritarian rule. Maithripala Sirisena, who defeated Mahinda Rajapaksa, says journalists can now work without intimidation and internet censorship will be lifted.

Sat 10th

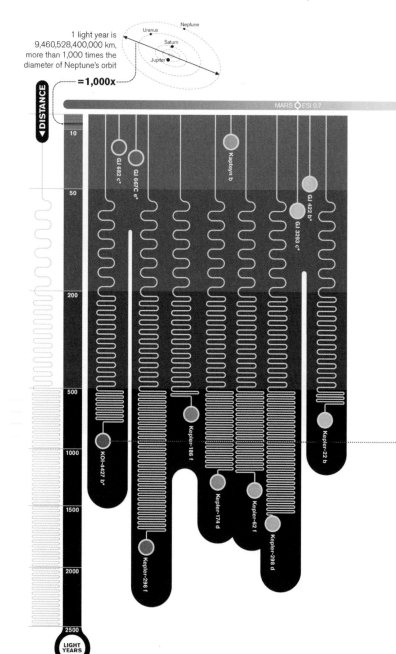

1 light year is 9,460,528,400,000 km, more than 1,000 times the diameter of Neptune's orbit

Neptune
Uranus
Saturn
Jupiter

=1,000x

◄DISTANCE

MARS ○ ESI 0.7

10

50

200

500

1000

1500

2000

2500

LIGHT YEARS

GI 682 c*
GI 667C e*
Kapteyn b
GI 422 b*
GI 3293 c*
KOI-4427 b*
Kepler-186 f
Kepler-22 b
Kepler-174 d
Kepler-62 f
Kepler-298 d
Kepler-296 f

Another Earth

New "Earth-like" planets were discovered in January, meaning there are now 30 known planets like home – but how long would it take us to get to them?

Source: HABITABLE EXOPLANETS CATALOG | Research: MARCUS WEBB | Illustrations: CHRISTIAN TATE

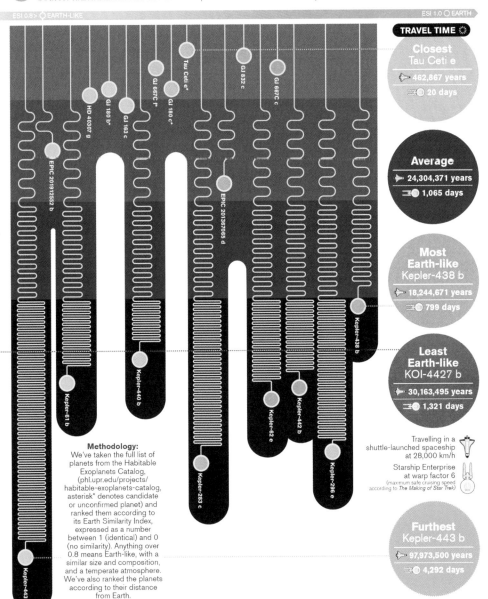

ESI 0.8> ○ EARTH-LIKE

ESI 1.0 ○ EARTH

TRAVEL TIME

Closest
Tau Ceti e
- 462,867 years
- 20 days

Average
- 24,304,371 years
- 1,065 days

Most Earth-like
Kepler-438 b
- 18,244,671 years
- 799 days

Least Earth-like
KOI-4427 b
- 30,163,495 years
- 1,321 days

Travelling in a shuttle-launched spaceship at 28,000 km/h

Starship Enterprise at warp factor 6
(maximum safe cruising speed according to *The Making of Star Trek*)

Furthest
Kepler-443 b
- 97,973,500 years
- 4,292 days

Planet labels (left to right / top to bottom): Tau Ceti e*, Gl 667C f*, Gl 180 c*, Gl 832 c, Gl 667C c, HD 40307 g, Gl 180 b*, Gl 163 c, EPIC 201912552 b, EPIC 201367065 d, Kepler-438 b, Kepler-61 b, Kepler-440 b, Kepler-62 e, Kepler-442 b, Kepler-283 c, Kepler-296 e, Kepler-443 b

Methodology:
We've taken the full list of planets from the Habitable Exoplanets Catalog, (phl.upr.edu/projects/habitable-exoplanets-catalog, asterisk* denotes candidate or unconfirmed planet) and ranked them according to its Earth Similarity Index, expressed as a number between 1 (identical) and 0 (no similarity). Anything over 0.8 means Earth-like, with a similar size and composition, and a temperate atmosphere. We've also ranked the planets according to their distance from Earth.

106.

What happens when the
speed of online news
dissemination outstrips reality?
Here's our pick of premature
conclusions, social media misfires
and hoaxes taken at face value.

Taken for a bride

It seemed like an outrageous tale of male stupidity and chauvinism: an Algerian groom sued his bride for damages the day after their wedding because she looked ugly without her make-up. According to the *Mail, the Mirror, the Express* and various other news sources, the groom saw his wife's natural looks the morning after their wedding and thought she was a burglar – and when he realised it was his wife he sued her for £13,000 in damages for causing untold psychological harm. The newspapers named as their source UAE newspaper *Emirates 24/7*, which itself credited unnamed "North African Arab newspapers" for the original story. It was, in fact, a single newspaper, *El Manchar*, which is Algeria's version of *The Onion*. *El Manchar*, which has a disclaimer on its site saying it's full of "completely absurd and false information", happily tweeted the news that its nonsense story was trending on social media.

Last to breaking news

A shocking story about a father in Dubai letting his drowning daughter die rather than have a male lifeguard touch her is, unfortunately, true. However, the dozens of media outlets worldwide that reported this story in early August were a little out of date – the incident took place in 1996. Again, the source was *Emirates 24/7*, which only clarified that its headline ("Dad lets daughter die, rather than be rescued by 'strange' rescuer") wasn't a recent incident in the final sentence of the article, with the line 'The incident happened many years ago'. Unless that last sentence was sneakily added by *Emirates 24/7* after its original publication in order to save face, it would appear that the journalists reproducing the story had a rather short attention span.

Snaps judgement

Numerous media outlets were fooled by an Instagram account purportedly belonging to Abdou Diouf, a Senegalese migrant who was using social media to document his perilous journey to Europe. Diouf seemed suspiciously social media-savvy, and cheery about his journey – a photo of him looking exhausted and miserable after a two-day walk in the summer heat is hashtagged #backpacker, #nature and #bored. Indeed, it wasn't real – it was a hoax designed to promote the Getxophoto festival in northern Spain. Diouf was played by Hagi Toure, a handball player who's lived in Barcelona for the past ten years.

Found on *delayedgratification.com*

107.

New research from Harvard Business
school suggests that the processes
involved with initiating and delivering
a sarcastic comment may improve the
creativity and cognitive functioning
of both the commenter and the recipient.
If you're friends.

"The study suggests that sarcasm has the potential to
catalyze creativity in everyone," said Francesca Gino, a professor of
business administration at Harvard University and a co-author of the study.
However, while the researchers agree that sarcasm and creativeness often
go hand-in-hand, Gino points out that it is possible that naturally
creative people may simply be more likely to use sarcasm,
making sarcasm the outcome, not the cause
of the relationship.

What do we think?
Sarcasm is overrated.
Even if it comes from a Japanese budgie.

popsci.com

108.

Back in the 70s and 80s it seemed that most grandparents
kept a budgie; a miserable, solitary creature destined to spend the rest
of its days in a cramped cage with nothing but a mirror and a piece
of cuttlefish for company. They were called either Joey or Peter,
regardless of sex. Perhaps there were a number of Pierres in Paris and
Piotreks in Poland. This Japanese version is for sale on
the Swearing Budgies site which hosts foul-mouthed poultry
from all over the globe. If you scan the QR code on the poster,
you can actually see what Petero is saying to you.
It's not nice.

swearingbudgies.co.uk

109.

The wall-mounted Wunder Wasser unit by **Francesco Faccin** draws influence from the wunderkammer, and functions as both a small place for personal objects, and a source of water. 'The simplicity of the structure and of the tap – very essential – is to make the content stand out. It is designed to be used in different environments where there is usually no water source, in a cozy bedroom, in an artistic studio, in a waiting room, in a corridor...'

francescofaccin.it

110.

'I became obsessed with
the simple idea of suspending
a seed on the surface of water;
submerged, just to the right level
for it to germinate. All with
the possibility of being able to
support itself in the absence
of soil, that would allow it
to stand upright; exposed,
all in clear view.'

The 'Mobile' of **Michael Anastassiades**
Floating Forest series balances
the seed.

studiomichaelanastassiades.com

111.

If you're in Jaipur, get photographed on the street by **Tikam Chand.**

Several years ago, I read about Tikam Chand, a photographer with a 1860s wooden box camera who sets up a simple photo studio daily on the sidewalk in Jaipur's Old City. I've been obsessed with the idea of it since. The studio location just down the road from Jaipur's honeycomb Hawa Mahal hasn't changed since his father and his grandfather were the ones behind the camera. Tikam Chand has been here for the past 18 years.

He smiles widely and calls out "One minute madam," as I walk in his direction. I don't need any convincing, I've been waiting for this for five years. His prints are available in three sizes. I choose the largest for Rs 300.

He lets me examine the camera, shows me what he sees inside, basically the subject upside down. He positions me on a stool based on his focal length and insists I don't move. There is no shutter release, he removes the cap from the gorgeous Carl Zeiss lens for two counts and puts it back on. The box camera has an inbuilt darkroom and the first step is producing a negative, which is rinsed with chemicals and then given a water bath. He affixes the negative to a board and photographs it to produce the final image. The end result is the perfect keepsake. A stunning portrait that looks as old as the camera itself. If you're in Jaipur, I couldn't recommend it more.

Note: An easy and worthy landmark for finding Tikam Chand is Pandit Kulfi, which sells ridiculously creamy, delicious kulfi. Tikam Chand can be found a block away in the direction of Hawa Mahal.

by Sheena Dabholkar on *thisissheena.com*
Sheena is a journalist and photographer who's work has been published in *The Wall Street Journal, stylus.com, Vogue, Lonely Planet, Mumbai Boss, Elle* and more. *Mumbai Boss* called her their "fave photog", *Nextness* included Sheena in their list of "vibrant innovative Asia blogs" and *Grazia* in their list of "scenemakers setting the tone for a changing cultural landscape". Bookmarking never seemed more appropriate.

112.

Kaffeeform is taking the phrase 'one man's trash is another man's treasure' to a whole new level with these coffee cups made from recycled coffee.

Having overcome the main challenge of making the cups washable
and hard-wearing enough to be reusable, Kaffeeform presents a genuine zero-waste
alternative for the ethically-minded consumer. The novel material has a number
of notable characteristics, the finished surface resembling the appearance of
dark marblewood grained with patterns unique to each piece. Even the smell
of coffee is retained in the finished cups.

What do we think?
People are embracing conscious consumption and upcycling is perhaps
the ultimate way to salvage even the most obscure waste.

113. 'I intervene in images by applying my own perception of beauty to them. Sometimes by giving them a new identity or a different aesthetic concept. It's the chance to give this image a new emotion, a new life, a new interpretation of beauty through embroidering.'

Jose Romussi

Jose Romussi

joseromussi.com

114.

Disturbing and provocative, the tongue-in-cheek work of artist duo
Fantich & Young plunges head-long into one of our time's most crucial and controversial
issues – that is, how a disproportionate amount of the world's wealth and power is in the
hands of a tiny elite and how everybody else is fighting to make it to the top. Designed for
"the discerning client with the taste for power and exclusivity", the brand's first collection aptly
named Apex Predator includes shoes, masks, two-piece ensembles, a perfume and other
accessories decorated with human hair, bones and thousands of human teeth (supposedly
collected after relentless headhunting on the steppes of neoliberal economics).

fantichandyoung.co.uk

Found at *yatzer.com*

115.

Izumi Miyazaki
transformed herself
from bored teenager to
Tumblr-sensation.

Noooo? How?
Her selfies using household items and
foodstuffs as props went viral.

Why?
The mix of her fixed, deadpan stare and
the intelligent styling makes this art.
There, we've said it.

Is it all bread-themed?
No.

izumimiyazaki.tumblr.com

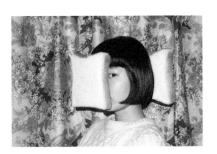

宮崎 いず美

116.

A one-suite hotel reminiscent of the belle époque, **Coqui Coqui Residence & Spa Merida** sits above the Coqui Coqui boutique and perfumery. Beyond the heavy velvet curtains lies L'Epicerie, a small café-style dining area situated in the backyard garden that lets you forget the Mexican heat as you indulge in handmade chocolate and freshly brewed coffee. Ex-model and owner Nicolas Maleville was inspired by the history of perfume in the Yucatan, when Franciscan monks worked closely with the indigenous Mayans to develop new and tropical scents for Spanish Royalty. Maleville (who has an academic and familial background in botany) founded and operates Coqui Coqui Perfumeria, while the Coqui Coqui Residences and Spas, Barberia and Boutiques are run alongside his wife Francesca Bonato. The Coqui Coqui lifestyle revolves around perfume but extends to an array of beauty products, including the most beautifully packaged shampoo, conditioner and toothpaste you'll ever own. Coqui Coqui's aesthetic combines Mayan tradition and Franciscan colonial style for a result that feels both masculine and feminine, primitive and luxurious.

Coqui Coqui Merida
Calle 55 516 entre Calle 62 y Calle 64, Centro,
97121 Mérida, YUC

coquicoqui.com

Found on *meltingbutter.com*

Text by Reemé Idris. All images courtesy of Coqui Coqui Merida.

117.

Gunnar Lillehammer is one of Germany's prominent street-style bloggers, and the main visual chronicler of the Munich art scene. The German-Swede had the first solo fashion blog exhibition in a German museum ever. We highly recommend you pick up a copy of Munich based art and fashion mag *Superpaper,* and you'll probably find a genre-defining editorial of Gunnar inside.

styleclicker.net

superpaper.de

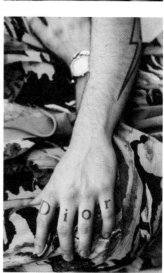

118.

We were tipped off on the work of **Ben Giles** by none other than Justin Timberlake.
And when Justin is a fan, we take a look. Artist, musician, occasional photographer and
self proclaimed 'enthusiastically bad dancer' Ben Giles likes to make people smile.
'I wouldn't say I set out to create humorous collages on purpose as I'm more interested in
pattern and colour and movement within my collages, but it's nice to make people smile though.'
And that is exactly what Justin Timberlake did when he picked a print of Giles for a charity event.
'That was cool,' says Ben. 'Collages are all about arranging the images from their pre-proposed
contexts and place into strange and rude new positions. It's really quick to make something funny
from existing images, it's like drawing risky facial hair on magazine covers, writing into dirty car
windows or rearranging fireplace ornaments into sexual positions, it's instantly gratifying.'

benlewisgiles.format.com

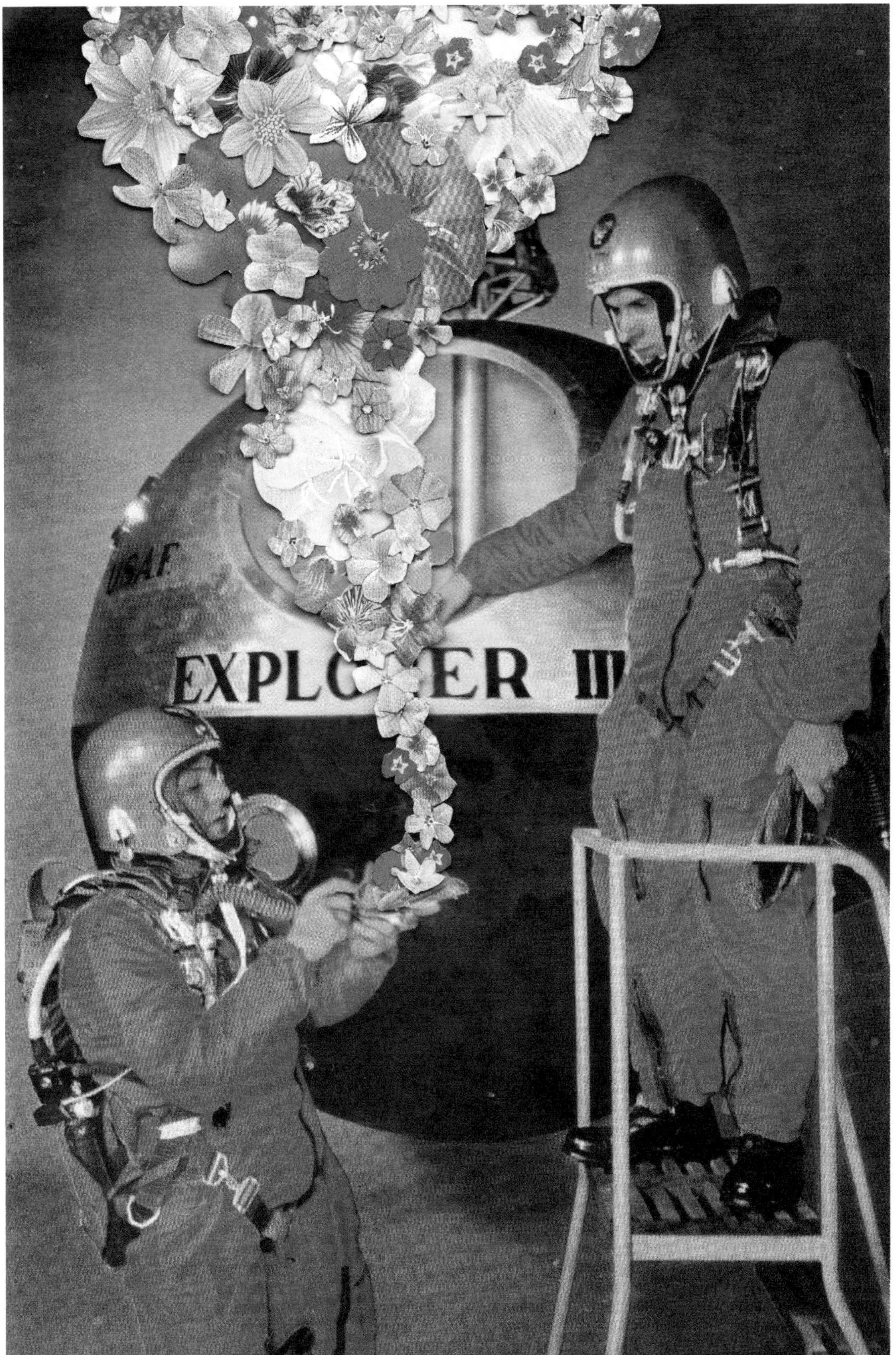
USAF
EXPLO ER III

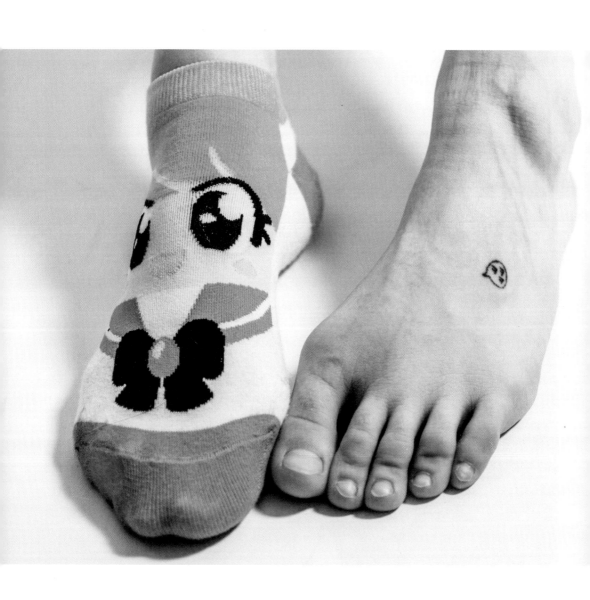

119.

'A lot of tattoo artists in Korea are working illegally, as you actually need a surgeon's licence to be allowed to tattoo.'

Who said that?

Codye Lazear, and American-born teacher/model/party organizer living in Seoul. Her friends gave her the Korean name *Kangnabi* (River butterfly), which she likes a lot.

What do we say?

We found Codye featured on *Tales in Ink*, the new project of Belgian- born photographer Rob Walbers. *Tales in Ink* shows amazing pics of people and their tattoos. 'Through the pictures and stories of the portraited people, we try to give an image of a city: Tokyo, Antwerp, London... All cities have different fashion trends, different concerns, different religions. In all these cities, people have different, or exactly the same reasons for getting tattoos,' says Rob. And guess what? 'Despite my profound interest in all things tattooed, I'm not tattooed myself. Never say never, but so far you can't find any ink on my body. Being afraid that once I start, I probably can't stop is one of the reasons! :-)'

Check out the rest of Codye's tatts at *blog.talesinink.com*

120.

Surprisingly, where the sun doesn't shine turns out to be an ideal setting for a garden. This Thai basil was grown 30 metres under the bustling shopping streets of London.

Over 30 metres below the bustling streets of London is a cavernous, abandoned space. Originally built to serve as a bomb shelter during World War II, it was designed to house and protect the lives of nearly 8,000 people. The space remained abandoned for close to 70 years until entrepreneurs Richard Ballard and Steven Dring decided to turn it into the world's first subterranean farm called **Growing Underground**. And surprisingly, where the sun doesn't shine turns out to be an ideal setting for a garden. The vertically stacked hydroponic beds are best for growing small, leafy greens that have a short growth cycle like watercress, Thai basil and Japanese mizuna. And with a state-of-the-art computer controlling temperature, lighting and nutrients the subterranean farm can deliver consistent produce without sunlight (or pesticides) and with 70% less water than conventional farms, hence the company's parent name: Zero Carbon Food. With the help of chef Michel Roux, the operation is now partnering with local restaurants to deliver farm-to-table produce in under four hours. Once fully operational, it's estimated Growing Underground will be able to produce between 5,000 to 20,000 kilos of crops annually.

thisiscolossal.com

121.

Japanese bookstore stocks only one book a week.

It can be hard for new publications to attract the attention of browsing customers in most bookstores. Despite beautiful covers and attractive displays, the sheer volume means any given book will only catch the eye of so many readers. Unless that is, the customer is browsing the new branch of **Morioka Shoten** in Japan – which only stocks one book at a time, each for a single week.

The store consists of a single room, containing a table – stocked with this week's publication, a chest of drawers – used as a counter, and a selection of art and objects relating to the book. Morioka Shoten hosts events every night of the week, except Mondays when the store is closed.

122.

Ode to Things is a tribute and
celebration of well-designed,
quality everyday objects run by an
artist-designer duo based in New England.
'We strive for an eclectic collection of
timeless designs. We stay away from trends,
gimmicks, and subcultures.
Our motto is a Duke Ellington quote:
"There are two kinds of music.
Good music, and the other kind."'

What do we say?
We need less stuff, better edited, so anyone taking time to
carefully choose a selection of high quality basics gets a polite
Yippee ki-yay, motherfucker from us.

odetothings.com

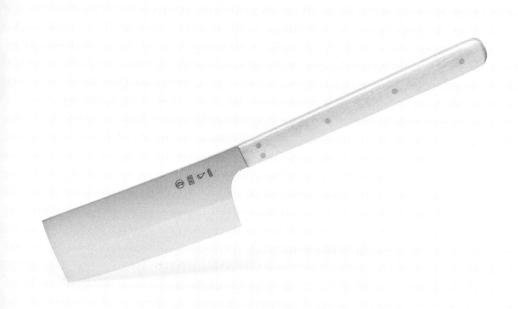

123.

Azmaya cheese knife

124.

This Pan/Vegetable brush is made by the Swedish company
Iris Hantverk which employs visually impaired craftsmen from a range
of cultures to manufacture their brushes. Perfect for cleaning pans and
vegetables in the kitchen, removing coffee grounds from your tablecloth,
or even sweeping away eraser residue from your drawingboard.

125.

A spurtle is a stirring utensil originally used in Scotland for porridge.
Its cylindrical shape allows the ingredients to be mixed without the dragging
effect of a spoon, preventing lumps that form during the process of cooking.
It stirs everything from soup to polenta. The Indeco spurtle is designed and
hand-crafted by Patrick and Mieke Senior-Loncin of Swan Point, Tasmania.
Thanks to its minimal and ornament-free outline, either end can be used;
for a quick mix vs. a precision stir.

odetothings.com

126.

Italian photographer **Sandro Giordano** delivers slapstick with a
fashionable twist. In his 'In Extremis (bodies with no regret)' series,
he captures the downfall of man. Be it mostly women positioned in haphazard,
awkward and unnatural positions, their abundant material belongings scattered
around them. Inspired by the artist himself falling from a bike, Giordano
takes a philosophical view on the images. 'My photographs are short stories about
a falling-down world. They tell the stories of people who live life at an
exhausting pace, experiencing sudden blackouts. When the demands of the modern
world become too much to cope with, our body rebels against our brain,
wreaking havoc in our day-to-day life.'
And it's funny.

@_remmidemmi

127.

With the advent of the yuccie – that is,
the Young Urban Creative – there's been a
slow demise of the hipster tribe, with millennials
now flocking toward more sophisticated shores.
They've now been adopted into the new
'creative class', and have opted for a cleaner,
sleeker look. That means banishing their
hoodies and flannels, becoming more
streamlined in their life choices, and leaving
behind that artefact of post-adolescence:
rebellious facial hair. **What was once seen
as the ultimate symbol of cool and the
quintessential sign of manliness is now
antiquated and unfashionable.**
Time to shave, boys.

128.

Dear God! There is a Ned Flanders themed metal band called **Okilly Dokilly.**

The world's first and only 'Nedal' band is bespectacled,
mustachioed, impeccably costumed in pink, green and grey,
and their Facebook bio gets straight to the point:
"Most of our songs are direct Ned quotes."

129.

Lake Hillier in Western Australia
is a lake that looks as if it's
been filled to the brim with
Pepto-Bismol.

The out-of-this-world body of water might seem
man-made and even toxic, but its bubblegum pink color is actually
entirely natural. Scientists have studied its composition, and, so far,
they've attributed the pink colour mostly to an algae that produces a reddish
beta-Carotene in salty waters. Lake Hillier is off-limits to visitors
but you can swim in other pink lakes nearby.

hillierlake.com/

130. **Hero** is the new buzz in Paris. A Korean inspired street-food and champagne hub in a pandemonium of tables made from strips of wood, marble, a peanut chopstick-holder, and a gorgeous sink in the middle of the room for washing your hands post chicken-devouring. Did we tell you about the chicken? It's all about yangnyeom: crispy fried chicken, covered in a sweet and sour garlic sauce or a spicy gochu jang sauce. Get there while it's hot.

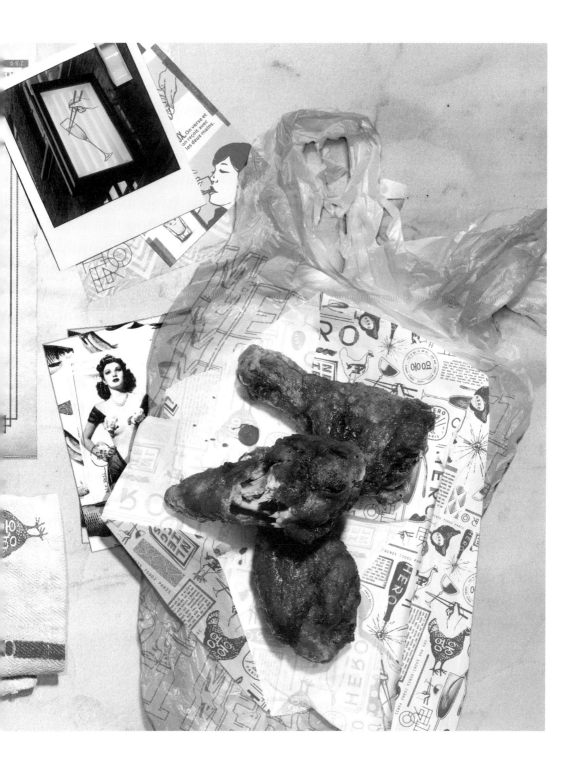

Restaurant Hero
289, rue Saint-Denis, Paris (75002)
heroparis.com

131. Bulging with annotated contacts and held together with packing tape, Frank Sinatra's oxblood leather social bible reads like a who's who of the jet set's golden age. A fortune cookie message affixed to the front cover reads, "Beware of friends, who are false and deceitful." The book, which the Chairman used and abused from the 1970s through the 1990s, recently sold at Julien's Auctions in New York City for the bargain price of $8,960.

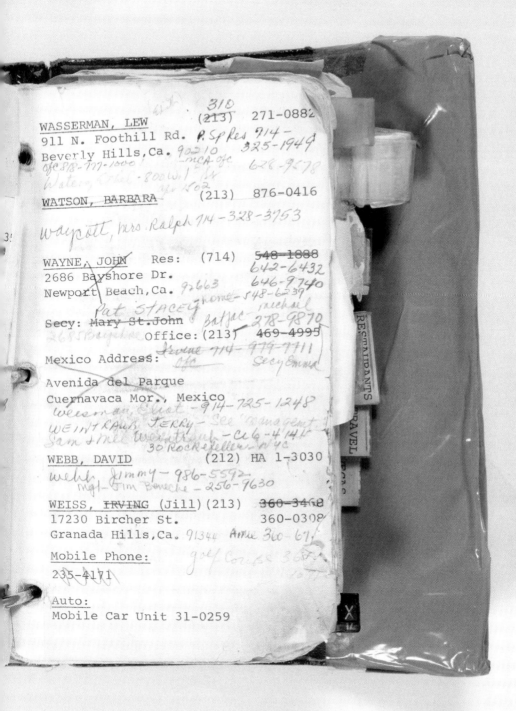

WASSERMAN, LEW   *310*   (213)   271-0882
911 N. Foothill Rd. *P. Spks 714-*
Beverly Hills, Ca. *90210*   *325-1949*
ofc 818-777-1000   *—MCA-Ofc*   *628-9578*
Waters, Ethel - 800 W. 1st Apt   *Apt #02*

WATSON, BARBARA   (213)   876-0416

Waycott, Mrs. Ralph 714-328-3753

WAYNE, JOHN   Res: (714)   ~~548-1888~~
2686 Bayshore Dr.   *642-6432*
Newport Beach, Ca. *92663*   *646-9740*
     Pat STACEY *home-548-6239*
Secy: ~~Mary St.John~~   *Batjac* *michael* *278-9870*
~~*2685 Bayshore*~~ Office: (213) ~~469-4995~~
Mexico Address: ~~*Irvine 714-979-7711*~~
     ofc   *Secy Emma*

Avenida del Parque
Cuernavaca Mor., Mexico
Weisman, Brut - 914-725-1248
WEINTRAUB JERRY— See "Management"
Sam & Mel Weintraub - CL6-4144
    30 Rockefeller - NYC
WEBB, DAVID   (212)   HA 1-3030
Webb, Jimmy - 986-5592
   Mgt-Jim Beneche - 256-9630

WEISS, ~~IRVING~~ (Jill) (213) ~~360-3468~~
17230 Bircher St.   360-0308
Granada Hills, Ca. *91344* *Anne 360-67*

Mobile Phone: *golf Course 367*
235-4171

Auto:
Mobile Car Unit 31-0259

132.

How many times have you gone to StreetFSN to admire the
street-style photography of **HB Nam** without knowing who he even is?
He's one of the leading street-style photographers right now with his very own
wacky Japanese brand-centric style. His blog is a regular
destination for eye-candy.

streetfsn.blogspot.de

@hbnam

133.

'A throwback to simpler days for the modern man'

NYTimes Style Magazine

Ok, a knife with a waiting list? Well, not just any knife. No two **Poglia knives** are the same. Each blade is hand-drawn and forged from repurposed steel, cut mostly from reclaimed disk plows. The handles are made from materials such as wood, horn and bone and are finished with solid brass.

Using ethical production methods and reclaimed resources, Max Poglia makes beautiful heirlooms that will stand the test of time. 'The knives, they can be a chef's knife, a steak knife, a utility knife. But the truth is, I love the idea of having a beautiful knife in my hand and going to the park to eat an apple.'

poglia.co

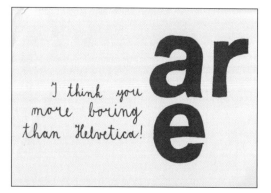

TODAY I SAW BULLSHIT AND GOT ANGRY ABOUT IT

134.

Slovenia-based illustrator
Kristjan Dekleva is a funny guy.
Check his Tumblr Linea Primitiva
for new uploads.

cickeracke.tumblr.com

drop

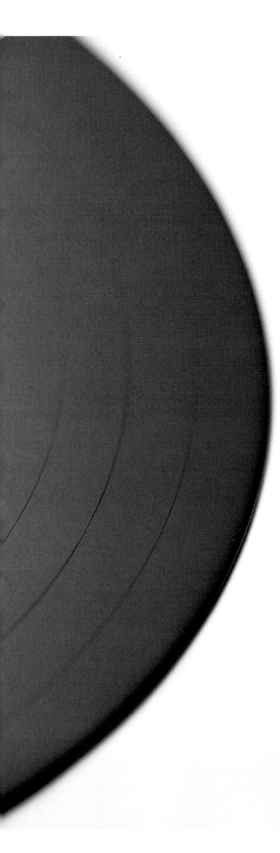

135.

This **Endless Rain record**
by Kouichi Okamoto
endlessly playing the
sound of rain drops is
perfect to put any
optimist in his place.

The grooves in the record form a circle which
makes it play longer then you will live.

kyouei-ltd.co.jp

136.

With **Where They Create**, the Australian photographer Paul Barbera changed his voyeurism into a sort of anthropological research.

'The blog is a visual project that documents the wonderfully diverse work spaces of creatives that I have met around the world. I'm an interiors and lifestyle photographer and I often travel, working with commercial and editorial clients. However, on these shoots, I usually collaborate with an editor or creative director who choose me to bring a certain kind of stylised 'look' for these spaces. Where They Create comes from a more personal and naturalistic style, where I take my voyeuristic tendencies and use them to examine the tools and objects that creatives accumulate in their studios over time.'

On this page, he shows the insides of one of his favorite online mags. 'Cool Hunting is a daily update on ideas and products ranging from art, design, culture and technology. This story could have been twice as long as their space is just filled to the brim with awesome trinkets. It was great to spend some time with the co-founders Josh and Evan. I first met them a few years ago at a dinner in Amsterdam while I was already a huge fan of their website.'

wheretheycreate.com

coolhunting.com

137.

Is there any small car on the market right now that is even remotely cute and timeless?

Hey Elon, stop building Maserati knock-offs and invest in a new car brand serving up vintage classics like this exceptional 1962 Heinkel Trojan with hybrid high-tech under the bonnet.

One of the sharpest three-wheeled whips in automotive history, this exceptional 1962 Heinkel Trojan is a conversation starter if there ever was one. Drool.

Where did we find this rare gem?

138.

We spotted the Trojan on *MAN of the WORLD No.10*, a quarterly handbook for the truly modern man founded by Alan Maleh in 2012. Maleh's publication goes beyond any tired cliché of luxury mags, and also offers a tightly curated selection of rare and vintage items for purchase. Their online journal has been one of our favorite hangouts for a while now.

manoftheworld.com

139.

Not Just A Label is rewriting the
rules of global fashion shopping.
With 539,000 unique visitors a month
and representing over 18,000 designers
from 110 countries, NJAL is the
world's leading designer platform
for showcasing and nurturing today's
pioneers in contemporary fashion.

Set up in 2008 to infuse new life into the fashion industry, NJAL quickly became
an indispensable tool for the industry; combating the hurdles that emerging talents face,
helping them gain exposure and financing their progression independently by providing an
easily accessible network and retailing forum. NJAL's products aren't lurking in a storage
facility or a factory floor. Every product a customer buys is delivered directly from the studio
of a young independent designer. Hand-packaged, hand-crafted, and helping emerging
design talents to support themselves wherever they are based in the world. The NJAL Shop
puts the power – and the profits – back into the hands of independent designers.
The concept cuts out the middle-men, creating a direct link between shopper and designer.
70% of a customer's spending directly funds the designers' progress and businesses worldwide,
supporting regional production and a more fair and ethical approach to fashion retail.
Apart from being the biggest young designer store on the globe, NJAL also hosts an
interesting selection of fashion films, features and interviews making this a
prime destination for anyone hungry for new fashion.

notjustalabel.com

140.

Large Fan Brush Earrings by **Niza Huang**
Inspired by paint brushes, these earrings are made for
maximum visual impact.

notjustalabel.com

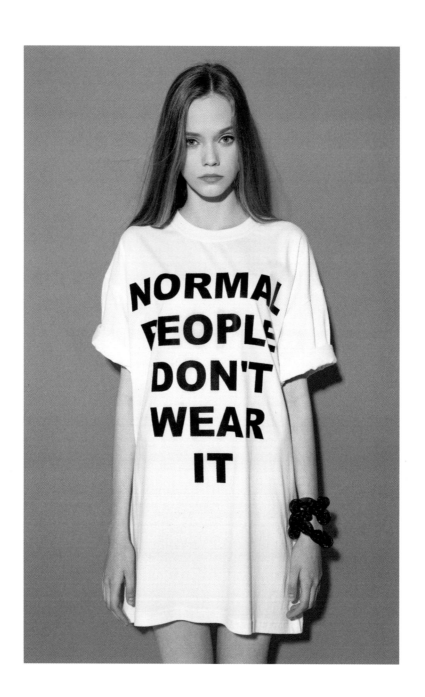

141.

Normal People T-Shirt by **Eleventen**
Oversize fit conversation starter par excellence.

notjustalabel.com

142.

Cobalto Trousers Medium Blue by **Fade Out Label**
This one of a kind trouser is made to order, and made from deconstructed
vintage jeans in shades of medium blue.

143.

A glimpse at any self-respecting design magazine will teach you that
cacti are all the rage. Connoisseurs will gladly tell you that this is all about an
esthetic and convenience perfectly fitted for the busy urbanite.
Next level plant experience are these New Realism paintings by Korean
artist **Kwang-Ho Lee**. His accurate renderings of the prickly plant become
ultra real even alien in Lee's environment. This has to do with the artist's
signature style which applies paint in an opaque manner to large canvases.
This gives the work a heightened sense of colour making
them more shocking and cinematic. Must-have.

johyungallery.com

144.

New Research Shows
How Spicy Foods Could Hold
The Key To Immortality.

After examining the diets of almost 500,000 people over a
seven-year period, researchers in China have recorded that those who
ate spicy foods once or twice a week had reduced their risk of death by
10% while those who ate such meals between three and seven days a week
had a 14% reduced risk of death – bridging links between the frequent
consumption of spicy food and longevity.

145.

Men who take selfies are more likely to show psychopathic traits.

Researchers at Ohio State University examined 1000 men
aged 18-40 and discovered that those who regularly post images
of themselves across social networking sites are more likely
to score highly on psychopath tests.

LARA STONE

146. **Sean Ryan** was shot to Insta-celebrity by making some of the most perfect faces on planet earth look like microwaved baseball mitts. It comes to no surprise that Sean's 'Badly Drawn Models' Instagram was vigourisly embraced by that arty fashion crowd that just loves that whole 'so bad it's good thing'-irony.

ANABEL KRASNOTSVETOVA

147.

Piccola Cucina Milan is a charming restaurant that is exactly as its name suggests. A tiny culinary gem accommodating only a handful of in-the-know Milanese who come with a robust appetite for traditional Italian cuisine cooked with a charismatic, contemporary twist and a good dose of finesse.

Piccola Cucina Milan
Viale Piave, 17, 20129 Milano, Italy

piccolacucina.it

Found on *meltingbutter.com*

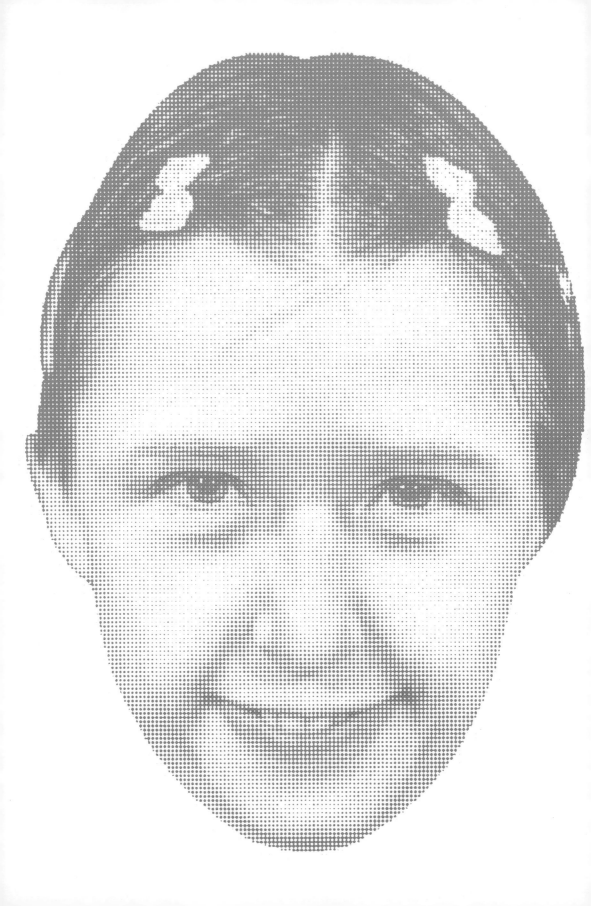

148.

Highbrow folk like us often find the traditional emoticon can struggle to express how we really feel.

We don't ALWAYS want to convey that we're
blindly happy, crying with laughter or
horizontally-lipped and nonplussed.
Sometimes, we need something a little more creative.
Thank the lord, then, that Hyo Hong has come up
with just the solution, in the form of the multifaceted
(in its truest sense) Cindy Sherman-icon.

itsnicethat.com

cindysherman-icon.tumblr.com

149.

There are many stunning, otherworldly sights in *Ex Machina*, the science-fiction film directed by Alex Garland that features a robot so lifelike she's played by actress Alicia Vikander. But the most breathtaking sight of all may be the 100 percent real, available-for-a-night's-stay location where the film is set: the **Juvet Landscape Hotel** in Norway.

Vanity Fair

What do we say?
Spending the night in a location of one of the best sci-fi pics in recent years is definitely on our must-do list. Much in contrast with the not so relaxing plot of the movie, the emphasis of the hotel is placed firmly upon awareness of the stunning surrounding environment, with each room sited and designed to maximise privacy whilst affording uninterrupted panoramic views. Each building has been designed in a responsive manner to its immediate environment – be it the sharp incline of a rock formation or lofty outcrop of surrounding forest.
It took location hunters a full-on global hunt to find the Juvet, but all you have to do is click on the link below.

juvet.com

Newport Beach - 1978
Maries Bike Shop

12/24/79 were
The Indis

150.

In the 1970s and '80s the Polaroid instant camera quickly captured family moments and delivered the images on the spot. Each snap is unique, and has no digital file or negative. Canadian artist **Kyler Zeleny** has over 6,000 of these in his Found Polaroids project, which is asking the public to create new narratives for the images with flash fiction, and to help track down the true stories behind the lost photographs.

foundpolaroids.com

151.

Everyone wants to be real these days.
When did authenticity become the
Holy Grail, I wonder?
The great irony is that, while all this
was happening, our daily lives were
becoming increasingly unreal. As mainstream
culture entered the digital age, we began to
socialise, shop, work and live in the abstract
for the very first time. It isn't a coincidence
that our cultural quest for a simple,
authentic ideal developed in
counterpoint into an increasingly complex,
globalised reality.

Henry Thoreau took himself off to live alone in rural Massachusetts 150 years ago. He wrote a book about the spiritual awakening created by his spartan, self-sufficient life in the woods. Despite his suspicions about technology (spoiler: he doesn't think much of the newfangled railway that threatens to disturb his peace and quiet), Thoreau was ahead of his time, right down to his hipster beard. "Real" became a commonplace compliment and aspiration in the Noughties. Jennifer Lopez sang about being it in 2001; Coca-Cola made it their slogan in 2003. The following year, Dove launched a "Campaign For Real Beauty", piggybacking on the vague but popular concept of the "real woman". The decade saw the dawning of the age of reality television: *Big Brother* launched in the UK in the year 2000. Fifteen years on, reality shows are still the most popular formats on TV, even though we know the narrative beats by heart. Social media has been a disruptive, democratising force – real voices are more valued, but this was accompanied by a shift in emphasis towards opinion, rather than reportage. It's about #realtalk, not information. The great irony is that, while all this was happening, our daily lives were becoming increasingly unreal. As mainstream culture entered the digital age, we began to socialise, shop, work and live in the abstract for the very first time. It isn't a coincidence that our cultural quest for a simple, authentic ideal developed in counterpoint to an increasingly complex, globalised reality.

To put it another way, as world events expanded and digitised themselves beyond the understanding of ordinary people, a contrary impulse kicked in. People began to yearn for something tangible – to prize the skill of the artisan, to hanker after the rough-hewn solidity of something made by a human hand. Men – lots of men – began to grow beards and dress like lumberjacks. Now there are Henry Thoureaus all over the country. In recent years, baking and craft have became a national obsession. Or, at least, watching other people bake and shopping for things that look crafty. Nostalgic *Keep Calm And Carry On* merchandise may be served with an ironic wink but, in an unpredictable world, its retro message is one we need to hear. Authenticity has become an industry. No area of life is exempt, even our minds – self-help books promise to show us how to lead authentic lives, as our authentic selves.

There are lots of pleasant, comforting things about all this. I like lovingly made food, the hiss of a secondhand record and tootling around by bike as much as the next North London ponce. I admire the skill and artistry of people who are good with their hands and who take care over the fine detail of their lives. I try to live what I consider to be an honest life. But I think our quest for authenticity has taken us off course. The #authenticity we're serving up these days is a corporate concept (if you want to depress yourself, look the hashtag up on Instagram). It is a £5 carrot juice. A pitch, a smug assertion of superiority, an unattainable ideal. It is a distraction. Authenticity, well… it isn't.

Luckily, there are lots of things that are better. I know this because I've long believed in keeping it unreal, ever since I became addicted to the glorious escapism of pop music as a little kid. As a music lover, I learnt very quickly that authenticity was a concept valued most by performers with the least imagination. Plus, I grew up in the North East, where nobody was interested in reality. Fantasy – the will to construct something better – was the aim. It was (is) considered polite to "make the best of yourself". Dressing up to the nines and heading out on Saturday night is pretty much obligatory. Years ago, this rich interior life brought meaning and beauty into an existence that was otherwise pretty hard. My grandad was a miner but, on the weekends, he was a club singer. There is still a boozer in South Shields where the correct answer to the pub-quiz question "Who sang *Unforgettable*?" isn't "Nat King Cole" but Bobby Gofton. That part of his life made him who he really was.

I'm sure authenticity has its place in politics but, for me, everyday life is best explained and experienced when it is refracted through the lens of imagination. Truth and facts are different, after all. Simple isn't necessarily better, nor should it always be the aim to strip things back. Each book I read and song I hear, every idea and experience, adds another layer of skin to the onion. As the horse says to The Velveteen Rabbit, "Real isn't how you are made. It's a thing that happens to you… you become. It takes a long time." I am still becoming, and I am not finished yet.

by Lauren Laverne.

Found at *the-pool.com*

152.

So this is what happens when
the former lead designer for BMW
and Peugeot decides to turn his
attention to creating an espresso
machine for the home?

'When you're a product designer, you think critically about
anything and everything around you. To imbue something
with originality is important, **Per Selvaag** explains. 'Honestly,
we're surrounded by great coffee; there's no void there.
So our goal, definitely, was to create a beautiful machine.'

What do we think?
Mission accomplished. This concrete home espresso machine
functions as both a work of art and a caffeine delivery system.
Where's the want button?

anzacoffee.com

70 x 50

'Sensibility'

"SENSIBILITY"

153.

'Our view of history is shaken. History only exists when someone writes it down. Memory doesn't exist, as it changes every time. *Game of Thrones*, which is a very successful TV series worldwide, is set in a fantasy world not related to any system – but the young people believe that this is how things really were. History is always invented by the person who is writing it down, who has the power to change it.'

Martin Eder in an interview in Zoo magazine

Despite or due to his Catholic upbringing in Bavaria, Augsburg-born artist, musician and photographer Martin Eder's describes his dedication to his art as "fundamentalist". Some people misinterpret his obsessive paintings as provocative, but according to Eder, they are definitely not. He creates a violent beauty in which reality is the scary part.
'In the past I used to plant spectacular elements into my paintings,' Eder says. 'I staged surreal and frightening situations, so people could see that something was obviously strange or wrong there. After a while, I drifted away from this approach because I trusted my paintings more. I learned that if you go back to reality it is frightening enough. If you show people one to one what's going on in the world, like in a mirror, it's even more frightening. At the moment, it's exactly the reality that is the disturbing element in my paintings.'

martineder.com

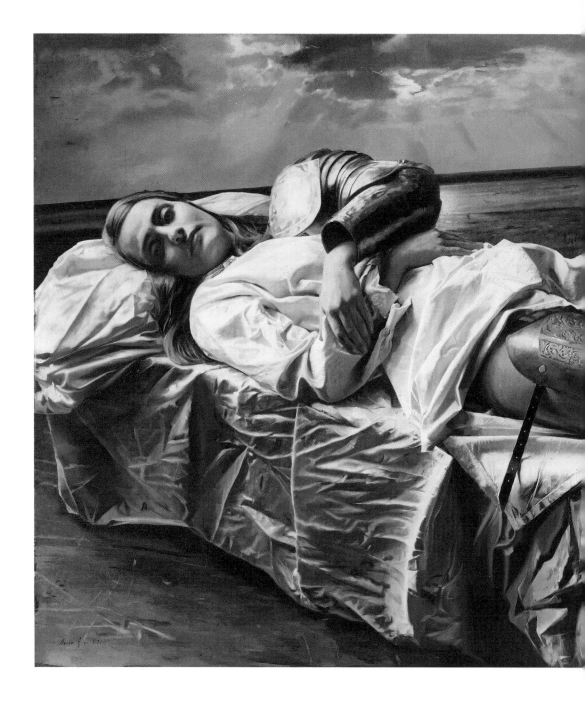

When Silence falls by **Martin Eder**
2015
225 cm x 150 cm.
oil on canvas

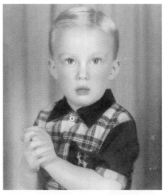

154.

'Looking back is never easy', the song says, but actually… we love it. Swiping through vintage pics is the closest we'll get to time travel (for now). Be it scary, giant babies, a 1930ies street scene in Cairo, a lion in the kitchen of Tippi Hedren (Who? Google her) or a selfie of a Belgian artist, this is eye-candy at it's best. Can you spot the guy running for president?

Plays like a flute ..
sounds like a
real bagpipe

$2¹⁴

It's Kenner's
Scottie Bagpipe

Play favorite Highland melodies like "Annie Laurie", "Campbells Are Coming", "Coming Thru the Rye" .. simple playing guides included. Inflate bag by blowing (valve won't let air escape). Then continue to blow gently and finger pipes to get exciting bagpipe effects. Plays automatically for 2 minutes after inflating. Can also be played as a woodwind without inflating. Red tartan plaid bag is made of sturdy vinyl, about 17x13 inches. Also has a flexible vinyl mouthpiece. Suitable for all ages.
49 N 568—Wt. 1 lb. 4 oz.....$2.14

155. With tree houses being all the rage, this spherical pod is the ultimate in hanging around.

While the fantasy of living in a treehouse may conjure up images of an idyllic lifestyle in the forest, not everyone is necessarily going to want to build their own shelter. For the more laid-back tree-loving adventurers amongst us, this **Cocoon Tree** is the answer. Weighing 60kg, the structure supports more than two tons above the ground. It's rigged up with ropes and secured by nets.

cocoontree.com

156.

There's no WiFi at
Satan's Coffee Corner,
so prepare to take some
time out and just
drink it all in.

Satan's Coffee Corner becomes all the more desirable thanks
to its clandestine location. Get ready to meander the back alleys of
El Barri Gòtic – into the depths of the urban warren, where no
tourists stray (thankfully!). And just as you think you've hit a
dead end, you might be lucky enough to stumble upon the café
you've been searching for. High ceilinged, bright and breezy,
this is one space that never fails to lift a black mood, with its
yellow furniture, azure walls, terracotta pots and cacti.
There's a menu of irresistible comfort foods and of course
proper coffee, served via a variety of brew methods, most likely
by a bearded hipster.

Satan's Coffee Corner
Carrer de l'Arc de Sant Ramon del Call, 11, 08002 Barcelona
satanscoffee.com/

Found on *meltingbutter.com*

Text by Nina Fitton. Photo by Misiska.

SEED MIXTURE

Harvest Noon

[11 am – 3 pm]

COLONI

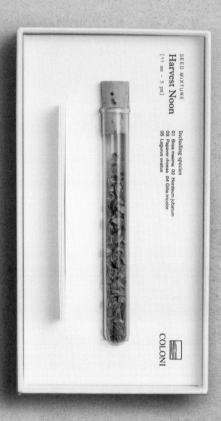

SEED MIXTURE

Harvest Noon

[11 am – 3 pm]

Including species
01 Briza maxima 02 Hordeum jubatum
03 Papaver rhoeas 04 Gilia tricolor
05 Lagurus ovatus

COLONI

157.

Coloni, a Swedish-based gardening house founded in 2010. In collaboration with a horticulturist, Coloni has developed an approach to a new kind of indoor gardening based on seed mixtures composed from a conceptual point of view. The mixtures consist of seeds from desert and arid Mediterranean climates and include both annual and perennial species. Indoor gardening by painting moods, we love it.

coloni.es

158.

Though P.T. Barnum made the Feejee
Mermaids famous, they were originally
created by Japanese East Indies fishermen
in around 1810. It was a traditional art form
in which they created faux mermaids by
stitching the upper bodies of apes to the
bodies of fish. P.T. Barnum began
exhibiting them in 1842, after a few other
showmen's exhibits failed.

What do we think?
Want.

Where?

What?

Who?

www.thelistmag.com

www.lannoo.com

Register on our website to regularly receive our newsletter
with new publications as well as exclusive offers.

Concept, curation & editing: Emm Verheyden
Book design & typeset: Bart Luijten

If you have any questions or remarks, do not hesitate to
contact our editorial team:
redactielifestyle@lannoo.com.

© Lannoo Publishing, Tielt, 2015
ISBN: 978 94 014 2915 3
Registration of copyright: D/2015/45/369
NUR: 450